CULTURES OF THE WORLD
Sri Lanka

mc Marshall Cavendish
Benchmark
New York

PICTURE CREDITS

Cover: © OmSriLanka/Alamy
AFP/Getty Images: 32 • Anders Blomqvist/Lonely Planet Images: 12, 29 • Asanka Brendon Ratnayake/Lonely Planet Images: 86, 111 • Christer Fredriksson/Lonely Planet Images: 1, 3, 16, 98 • Christian Aslund/Lonely Planet Images: 15 • Dallas Stribley/Lonely Planet Images: 44, 72, 97 • Getty Images/Photolibrary: 10 • Greg Elms/Lonely Planet Images: 60, 96, 113, 126 • Inmagine: 6, 11, 13, 17, 18, 24, 26, 36, 45, 46, 52, 57, 75, 103, 110, 124, 127, 130, 131 • Ishara S. Kodikara/AFP/Getty Images: 47 • John Borthwick/Lonely Planet Images: 30, 67 • Juliet Coombe/Lonely Planet Images: 66 • Kevin Clogstoun/Lonely Planet Images: 5, 14, 51, 59, 70, 71, 76, 79, 80, 82, 87, 90, 92, 93, 105, 106, 112, 116, 120, 121 • Kimberley Coole: 8 • Lakruwan Wanniarachchi/AFP/Getty Images: 37, 39, 114 • Michel Baret/Gamma-Rapho/Getty Images: 49 • Mick Elmore/Lonely Planet Images: 78 • Oliver Strewe/Lonely Planet Images: 22, 25, 27, 48, 53, 56, 63, 88, 107, 119, 128 • Ray Tipper/Lonely Planet Images: 61 • Richard I'Anson/Lonely Planet Images: 74, 102, 104 • Robert Nickelsberg/Time Life Pictures/Getty Images: 41 • Scott Eells/Bloomberg/Getty Images: 38 • Sena Vidanagama/AFP/Getty Images: 64, 69

PRECEDING PAGE

Two children enjoying a bicycle ride on their way to Wilpattu National Park.

Publisher (U.S.): Michelle Bisson
Writers: Nanda Pethiyagoda Wanasundera, Jo-Ann Spilling
Editors: Deborah Grahame-Smith, Stephanie Pee
Copyreader: Tara Tomczyk
Designers: Nancy Sabato, Khandadai Shankar Adithi
Cover picture researcher: Tracey Engel
Picture researcher: Joshua Ang

Marshall Cavendish Benchmark
99 White Plains Road
Tarrytown, NY 10591
Website: www.marshallcavendish.us

Library of Congress Cataloging-in-Publication Data
Wanasundera, Nanda P. (Nanda Pethiyagoda), 1932-
 Sri Lanka / Nanda Pethiyagoda Wanasundera, Jo-Ann Spilling. — 3rd ed.
   p. cm. — (Cultures of the world)
 Includes bibliographical references and index.
 ISBN 978-1-60870-994-6 (print) — ISBN 978-0-7614-0001-1 (eBook)
 1. Sri Lanka—Juvenile literature. I. Spilling, Jo-Ann. II. Title.

DS489.W25 2013
954.93—dc23   2011042595

Printed in Malaysia
7 6 5 4 3 2 1

CONTENTS

SRI LANKA TODAY

THE ANCIENT NAME FOR SRI LANKA IS SERENDIP—A NAME THAT inspired the word *serendipity*, meaning to find something that you do not expect to find. The English author Horace Walpole, who coined the name, also wrote a fairy tale entitled "The Three Princes of Serendip" in which the heroes keep making accidental discoveries during their travels. The name and the accompanying fairy tale are highly fitting for this magical and paradisiacal island that has come to be known, since 1972, as Sri Lanka. In spite of earlier decades of war and conflict, those who are fortunate enough to visit this land are astounded by Sri Lanka's stunning natural beauty, its scenic landscapes, multifarious sounds, and exotic smells, and, last but not least, the warm smiles and friendly faces of its people.

Although it is only a compact little island, this unique teardrop-shaped nation has a kaleidoscope of attractions and experiences—natural, historical, and cultural—to offer its visitors.

The mountains are spectacular, the coasts boast beautiful beaches, and the forests are full of biodiverse wildlife, and unique flora and fauna. Parts of the coastline are still recovering from the devastating tsunami that battered the southern, eastern,

The beautiful Rawana Falls.

and northern parts of the island on Boxing Day (December 26) in 2004. This "jewel" of an island is home to valuable blue sapphires, cat's eyes, and other precious stones, especially produced in the city of Ratnapura. Other treasures that tell of the island nation's past can be found in the ancient cities of Anuradhapura, Polonnaruwa, and the rock fortress of Sigiriya. Nature can be appreciated by visiting Sri Lanka's impressive waterfalls and lush green tea plantations. Its abundant natural beauty, ancient customs, and traditions intermingle comfortably with modern life, which can be observed in the vibrant capital city of Colombo as well as in other major cities and towns.

The ordinary lives of many Sri Lankans have in the recent past been inevitably shaped by the 26-year-long civil war with the Tamil Tigers, which killed more than 70,000 people. Fortunately the conflict finally came to an end in May 2009 when government forces seized the last area controlled by the Tamil Tiger rebels. In spite of the conflict, Sri Lankans from different ethnicities and religious beliefs have always tried to live peacefully with one another. The essence of Sri Lankan culture derives from the key facets of the major religions practiced in this country—Buddhism, Hinduism, Islam, and Christianity—all of which promote peace and tolerance.

Travelers to Sri Lanka bear witness to this tranquil attitude as they receive a friendly welcome followed by gentle hospitality. Sri Lanka's traditional welcome, *Ayubowan* (meaning "Long may you live"), is genuinely extended to each and every visitor. Visitors will observe that, irrespective of their ethnic background, Sinhalese, Tamil, and Muslim locals will welcome them with pride—pride in their delicious cuisine, pride in their national parks and wildlife, and, especially, pride in their national cricket team.

This strong sense of national pride apart, Sri Lankans are generally a relaxed people. For instance, timekeeping can be a loose concept, and deadlines, appointments, and meetings are regularly late, delayed, and sometimes missed altogether. Except for the efficient train network, which runs like clockwork, it is uncommon for the majority of Sri Lankans to begin or complete anything punctually or to manage to meet at the pre-agreed time. This laidback approach to life can also be seen in the way in which Sri Lankans value and enjoy their leisure time with friends and family. In the cities and bigger towns, many indulge in sporting activities as well as going shopping or to the cinema.

Sri Lankans' easy and kind manner can also be observed in the way people, animals, and vehicles seem to coexist in relative harmony. It is common to see animals such as cows, goats, and dogs wandering aimlessly across busy roads and basking in the sun on pavements and even on beaches, while people go about their daily business. The towns and cities bustle with people everywhere—walking, cycling, traveling in a *tuc-tuc* (took took) vehicle (a three-wheeled auto rickshaw), by motorbike, in a taxi, bus, car, or truck— each striving to reach their destination. Even when there is heavy traffic congestion, most Sri Lankans remain polite and only occasionally express real annoyance. It appears that even though people in Sri Lanka are generally poorer than their Western counterparts, they seem content. Many visitors and expatriates who live and work in Sri Lanka are enticed by the slower pace of life, and as a consequence, they adopt a simpler lifestyle when living there.

Although many Sri Lankans are caring and sociable, it is not normally conventional to show public displays of emotion such as anger or affection. Even though Western manners and dress styles are being adopted by many urban Sri Lankans today, especially among the younger generation, certain formalities and traditions still remain important. For example, women are expected to dress conservatively and Western ways of greeting such as kissing and hugging are not usually acceptable.

Irrespective of their ethnicity and religious backgrounds, the role of the majority of women living and working in Sri Lanka today remains mainly traditional. However, in the urban centers and among the more educated, this attitude is gradually changing.

Within the typical Sri Lankan family, women perform distinct household duties such as looking after the children, cooking, cleaning, and washing.

A Sri Lankan woman picking tea leaves.

Women in rural families have to help with farming and other agricultural activities such as harvesting. Poorer women in Sri Lanka often engage in full-time or part-time jobs, looking after the household chores of more wealthy families. Many middle-class women pursue their education and find work until they get married. Like in other traditional cultures, men are the heads of their families and are generally expected to protect and provide for them.

In the 1970s Sri Lankan women started to seek employment abroad, driven by the lack of employment opportunities at home and compounded by factors such as debt and other domestic problems. The number of women migrant workers has increased rapidly, and today it is estimated that more than 1.7 million of them work in foreign countries. Most of them are employed as domestic housemaids in the Middle East in countries including Saudi Arabia, Kuwait, Lebanon, the United Arab Emirates, and Qatar.

After many years of working abroad, some of these women are able to return home with enough savings to build their own houses and even set up their own small businesses. In an attempt to reduce the number of women who need to seek employment abroad, away from their home and families, the Sri Lankan government has established several projects to support poorer women and provide them with opportunities in industries such as dressmaking, food manufacturing, and even tourism.

Although many do not like to admit it, caste and social class still play a significant role in Sri Lankan politics and economics, and life in general. This is not so obvious in urban society, but in rural areas, it is still common to see segregation of people based on caste.

In daily life, the caste divisions are not easily discernible, and people from different classes freely interact with one another at work and in social situations. Modern urban life, particularly in big cities such as Colombo where people of different castes are forced to intermingle on the streets and on public transportation, makes enforcing the divisions of caste impractical.

Although the caste system has been officially eliminated and equal opportunities exist in employment, health, and education, subtle forms of prejudice continue to exist in certain areas such as within political organizations. Intermarriage between couples of different castes is still quite rare in Sri Lanka, although it does take place. To maintain caste purity, the majority of marriages in both urban and rural communities take place between a man and a woman of the same caste.

In rural areas caste divisions are less invisible. Differences are enforced by the manner in which people of different castes greet and speak to each other. For example, an individual's caste can be ascertained simply by the name he has been given. A person from a high caste will be greeted with a formal title. In certain traditional villages, communities are segregated into separate areas according to their castes.

For all of Sri Lanka's cultural treasures and natural riches, it must be said that despite the tensions of the caste system, the resilient spirit and compassion of its ordinary people are its greatest assets. The proof of this lies in the fact that, in spite of a painful history of civil war, the horror of the 2004 tsunami, and the recent 2008 global financial crisis, Sri Lankans continue to be positive, optimistic, and determined to improve their everyday lives.

Many parts of Sri Lanka are still largely untouched and unaffected by mass Western tourism, but this is changing fast, particularly with the welcome end of the long civil war in 2009. Recently the *New York Times* announced that Sri Lanka was on top of the list of places to visit in 2010. As a result tourism is steadily growing, and as more and more people become acquainted with the country's exquisite beauty, Sri Lanka will very soon be a desirable destination.

Blessed with a combination of breathtaking scenery, an interesting and ancient culture and history, a harmonious society, and a stable economy, the resplendent isle of Sri Lanka is beginning to make its mark on the world stage.

GEOGRAPHY

Vegetation covering the cliff face at World's End in Horton Plains National Park.

1

ROUGHLY THE SHAPE OF A PEAR, Sri Lanka covers an area of 25,332 square miles (65,610 square kilometers), approximately half the size of Alabama. The island measures 140 miles (225 km) at its widest and 270 miles (435 km) from Point Pedro in the north to Dondra Head in the south.

Sri Lanka lies just 30 miles (48 km) south of India, with which it shares the same continental shelf. Romantics call Sri Lanka the "Teardrop of India." To the island's south is the vast Indian Ocean, and to the east is the Bay of Bengal. In distant years past, Sri Lanka's position was

The coast along the city of Matara, the southernmost point of Sri Lanka.

The Mahaweli River is vital to Sri Lanka. The country's longest river has a massive drainage basin covering approximately one-fifth of the total area of the island. A total of six dams are connected to the Mahaweli system, providing over 40 percent of Sri Lanka's electricity needs.

strategically important, located on the major sea routes that linked Asia with Europe, the Middle East, and Africa.

PARADISE BORN OF UPHEAVALS

Geologists believe that Sri Lanka once lay beneath the sea. A series of earthquakes probably thrust the land up, producing an island with south-central hills crowned with mountains that slope sharply into valleys. Plains stretch out in the north toward the Jaffna Peninsula.

Sri Lanka's highest point is a mountain near the town of Nuwara Eliya. Pidurutalagala stands at 8,281 feet (2,524 meters).

RIVERS, FALLS, AND TANKS

Most of Sri Lanka's rivers begin in the south-central hills and flow outward to the sea, tumbling over rocky precipices on the way and forming waterfalls.

Sri Lanka's longest river is Mahaweli Ganga at 208 miles (335 km), and its shortest is Gal Oya at 67 miles (108 km). The island's most famous

The Mahaweli Ganga River, whose name means "great sandy river" in Sinhalese.

LEGENDS OF THE FALLS

Sri Lanka's grand waterfalls have inspired poets, painters, musicians, and storytellers.

The turbulent waters of the Dunhinda plunge from a height of 200 feet (61 m) into a large deep pool, where legend has it that a beautiful fish wearing a golden earring swims. The story goes that the fish swims over the buried treasure of Kumarasinghe, the prince of Uva, and comes to the surface only once a year. Legend also has it that the treasure is guarded by men armed with gold swords. Those who swim in the pool must beware, as the guardians of the treasure look for a human sacrifice every year.

A romantic legend associated with the Dunhinda tells of a princess from the Gampola Dynasty who eloped with her commoner lover. The unfortunate couple was tracked down to a village near the falls. Determined not to be separated, the couple fled to the highest ledge of the Dunhinda and jumped to their deaths. The same night, a terrible storm wiped out the surrounding villages. Even today, people say that they still hear the lovers' shrieks when storms reach their peak.

Lover's Leap in Nuwara Eliya has its source in the Pidurutalagala mountain. This waterfall is believed to be haunted by the ghosts of another runaway couple; they jumped to their deaths to avoid an angry father.

The Ravana near Ella is named after the villain of the Ramayana epic. According to legend, the evil king Ravana once lived in a cave near this waterfall.

Bridal Falls is the name given to Saint Clair Falls in Talawa-kele, because its waters resemble a bride's veil.

Baker's Falls is named after its discoverer, Sir Samuel Baker, the British explorer who mapped the upper Nile. At Nuwara Eliya, Baker set up an experimental farm, where he introduced English vegetables.

Victoria Dam is the largest hydroelectric source in Sri Lanka.

waterfalls are the Dunhinda and the Diya-luma. The latter gets its name from the Sinhala word *diyahaluma* (DI-yah-loo-meh), which means "spilling waters." Sri Lanka's highest waterfall is the Bambarakanda, with a fall of 863 feet (263 m).

The rivers of Sri Lanka were tamed by the Sinhalese kings. Through feats of hydraulic engineering, the kings created artificial lakes and turned arid scrubland into fertile fields, earning Sri Lanka the title of "Granary of the East." Some of Sri Lanka's man-made lakes, called tanks, date from the Anuradhapura period over 2,000 years ago. Currently 10 large hydroelectric power stations are in operation, all between 38 and 210 megawatts (a megawatt is a unit of electrical power), with the Victoria Dam being the largest hydroelectric source.

CLIMATE

Sri Lanka has a tropical climate. It is hot and wet through most of the year. Humidity is high in some places, making the daytime unpleasant, though the nights are relatively cooler. Temperatures in the coastal regions range

Rainfall across Sri Lanka varies from region to region.

between 80°F and 83°F (27°C and 28°C). Temperatures in the northwest of the island can reach 100°F (38°C) and higher, while in the south-central hill country, the temperature hovers around 50°F (10°C). The average annual temperature for the country as a whole ranges from 82.4 to 86°F (28 to 30°C).

The hottest months are March and April, while the driest month is February. From December to January, the entire island enjoys a break from the tropical heat, and the hill country experiences an almost temperate climate.

Rainfall in Sri Lanka varies considerably from one region to the next. The central highlands receive the most rainfall, especially on the western slopes, where annual measurements of more than 200 inches (500 centimeters) have been recorded. The eastern slopes receive significantly less rain— less than 138 inches (350 cm) annually.

The northwestern and southeastern lowlands receive the least rain. Rainfall in the north averages 40 inches (100 cm) annually, and up to 200 inches (500 cm) of rain falls in the southwestern mountains. The average rainfall is about 200 inches (508 cm) in the south-central hills and 75 inches (191 cm) in the north and east of the island.

There are two monsoon seasons each year. The southwest monsoon, active from May through August, is the main rain-giver. It waters Sri Lanka's wet zone, which includes the western, southern, and central hills facing the moisture-laden southwesterly winds. After shedding its moisture, the dried-out winds blow across the eastern plains. The northeast monsoon waters the northern and eastern parts of the country from October through January. It brings less rain than the southwest monsoon, though it can sometimes cause floods.

EVERYTHING IS GREEN

A visitor's first impression of Sri Lanka likely includes how green the island is. Trees in varied shades of green abound, and against the fresh green of leaves blazes the brilliant crimson of bougainvillea and flame-of-the-forest flowers.

Sri Lankan flora ranges from the mangroves on the coast and the dense tropical evergreen rain forest of the lowland wet zone to the thorny trees of

A stream cutting through the tropical rain forest in Kanneliya Forest.

the dry zone and the tough grasslands called *patana* (PAH-teh-neh), dotted with red rhododendron.

The primeval Sinharajah forest, with its tall trees and thick undergrowth, is home to the fast-disappearing Vesak orchid and is now a protected area. Much land has been given to agriculture and forestry, and deforestation has left a clear mark on Sri Lankan soil.

ANIMAL LIFE

Sri Lanka is well known for its bountiful wildlife, although extensive land cultivation has forced many animals to retreat to the confines of the few remaining forests on the island.

There are 91 species of mammals living in the safety of the national parks, which include the Asian elephant, the sambar, spotted leopard, sloth bear, black-faced langur, reddish-brown macaque, purple-faced leaf monkey, elk, barking deer, spotted deer, and mouse deer. The 171 species of reptiles include the saltwater crocodile, leatherback turtle, iguana, and

The blue magpie, also known as the Ceylon magpie, is endemic to Sri Lanka.

Colombo, the capital city of Sri Lanka.

several species of snake, including the deadly cobra and saw-scaled viper. Most of Sri Lanka's 82 species of fish live in the inland marshes and rivers. Rainbow and brown trout swim in the cold waters of the Horton Plains.

More than 227 species of indigenous and migrant birds have been sighted in Sri Lanka, although some claim that there are as many as 400 species. Among the endemic species are the Ceylon blue magpie, Layard's parakeet, and chestnut-backed owlet. There are also barbets, flycatchers, and thrushes. In the Ruhuna (popularly called Yala) National Park, the peacock performs its mating dance during the months from December to May. Ruhuna—a semi-arid, thorny scrub forest in the southeast—is the country's largest national park after Wilpattu—a lush, thick secondary forest in the northwest. Three other national parks in Sri Lanka are the Gal Oya, Uda Walawe, and Lahugala. At the Lahugala Tank in Lahugala National Park, elephant grass grows wild. Herds of wild elephants are drawn to this sanctuary during their migration through the island.

CITIES

COLOMBO Sri Lanka's capital, Colombo, is located on the western coast. The harbor bustles with merchant and cargo vessels, and the international airport at Katunayake is just 30 minutes away from the city. The Galle Face Green promenade has many large hotels, the most famous being the more than 150-year-old Galle Face Hotel. Colombo has a population of more than 1.3 million and is divided into 15 postal districts. Slums sit alongside five-star hotels and palatial private residences. The center of the city and its commercial hub is the Fort, a Dutch fortification and the site of the president's residence. Other famous landmarks include the two World Trade Center towers, the Bank of Ceylon, the Old Parliament Building, the Old Colombo Lighthouse, Independence Hall, Jami Ul-Alfar Mosque, and Saint Paul's Church, Milagiriya.

A few miles to the east of Colombo lies Kotte, the ancient royal capital, where the new parliamentary complex stands in the Diyawanne Oya at Sri Jayewardenepura.

KANDY Declared a World Heritage site by UNESCO in 1988, Kandy is the home of "The Temple of the Tooth Relic" (*Sri Dalada Maligawa*), making it one of the most important places of pilgrimage for Buddhists all over the world.

JAFFNA Most Sri Lankan Tamils have their roots in Jaffna, the major battle ground of the terrorist group, the Liberation Tigers of Tamil Eelam, or LTTE. Desiring a separate state for Tamils, the LTTE started a civil war in Jaffna and ruled the peninsula before government forces regained control in 1996. The road through the Wanni region, the stronghold of the LTTE, used to be dangerous. Tamils going home to see their relatives had to travel by air or sea, while tourists visiting Jaffna had to travel with military escort. However, since the end of the civil war in 2009, many refugees have returned to their homes to support the reconstruction and regeneration of the city.

GALLE AND TRINCOMALEE Galle on the southwestern coast and Trincomalee to the northeast are natural harbors. Both have Dutch fortresses and a quaint, sleepy air. Trincomalee is the site of a major historical attraction, Swami Rock. The ruins of a Hindu temple sit squarely on a cliff that drops into the deep blue sea. Closenburg in Galle is a swimmer's paradise.

NUWARA ELIYA Nestled in the hill country, Nuwara Eliya is the gem of Sri Lanka's hill resorts. Remnants of British colonial influence are still seen in the colonial buildings and gardens. Nur'Eliya, as it is locally known, is also famous for its tea plantations.

INLAND TRAVEL

Railroads connect Sri Lanka's cities. The trains are clean, reliable, and not overcrowded. Intercity vans and minibuses, on the other hand, are always jam-packed, with passengers hanging precariously at the doors.

Barges and outrigger canoes called catamarans navigate the canals radiating from Colombo. For those in no hurry, a cart drawn by an ox or a team of oxen ambles along, speeding up only when goaded by a sharp jab of the carter's stick. Mercifully the rickshaw, with its human beast of burden, is no longer a mode of transportation.

Road travel in the towns and suburbs is usually a noisy, and often hair-raising, experience. Carefree cyclists, motorbike maniacs, horn-tooting motorists, overloaded buses, and nonchalant jaywalkers contribute to the general mayhem.

In the less populated and more remote rural areas, however, newly paved roads offer a smooth ride, and even the older roads riddled with ruts, humps, and potholes are easy to travel, since they are comparatively free of traffic.

ADAM'S PEAK

Sri Pada, or Adam's Peak, is a conical rock rising 7,360 feet (2,243 m) in the south-central hills. On clear days, Adam's Peak can be seen even from Colombo on the western coast. At night, from December through March, Adam's Peak is visible from miles away, a string of lights reaching toward the sky. The lights mark a steep path up the mountain slope.

Christians, Muslims, Buddhists, and Hindus venerate Adam's Peak. On the summit is a mark in the rock that is the shape of a giant footprint. Muslims say it is Adam's footprint, which he left there when God banished him from Eden; hence the name Adam's Peak. Christians believe it is the footprint of Saint Thomas, the apostle who brought Christianity to Sri Lanka. Buddhists believe the Buddha left his footprint on the summit during his final visit to Sri Lanka. And Hindus say the footprint is that of god Shiva. Further enhancing its religious role are the structures on Adam's Peak: a *dagoba* (DAH-go-beh), or Buddhist temple, a shrine, and a temple to the god Saman.

The most popular route for pilgrims and tourists climbing to the summit is a 2-mile (3-km) climb through tea estates and rocky terrain, followed by another 2-mile trek up sheer rock-hewn steps. On the way, the trekker passes a Japanese peace shrine (stopping to discard a needle and a ball of thread for luck), souvenir stands, and restrooms. Even water is sold, the price escalating as one's climbing stamina decreases!

Most people climb through the night in order to reach the summit at dawn—in time for the spectacular sunrise that throws the shadow of the peak for miles beyond. The amazing thing is that the pinnacle can accommodate so many people. A bell tolls continuously as pilgrims register the number of times they have climbed Adam's Peak by giving the bell-rope the corresponding number of tugs.

INTERNET LINKS

www.citypopulation.de/SriLanka.html

This site provides comprehensive population figures on the districts of Sri Lanka as well as all cities, including municipal councils and urban councils, of more than 20,000 inhabitants.

www.internationalrivers.org/south-asia/sri-lanka

This is the official website of International Rivers—an organization that protects rivers and defends the rights of communities that depend on them. It has coverage of Sri Lanka's water-related issues, including its long history of irrigation and water development projects.

www.mapsofworld.com/sri-lanka/geography/

This website provides valuable information about the geography of Sri Lanka, including details and links to its location, topography, demographics, weather, map, and cities.

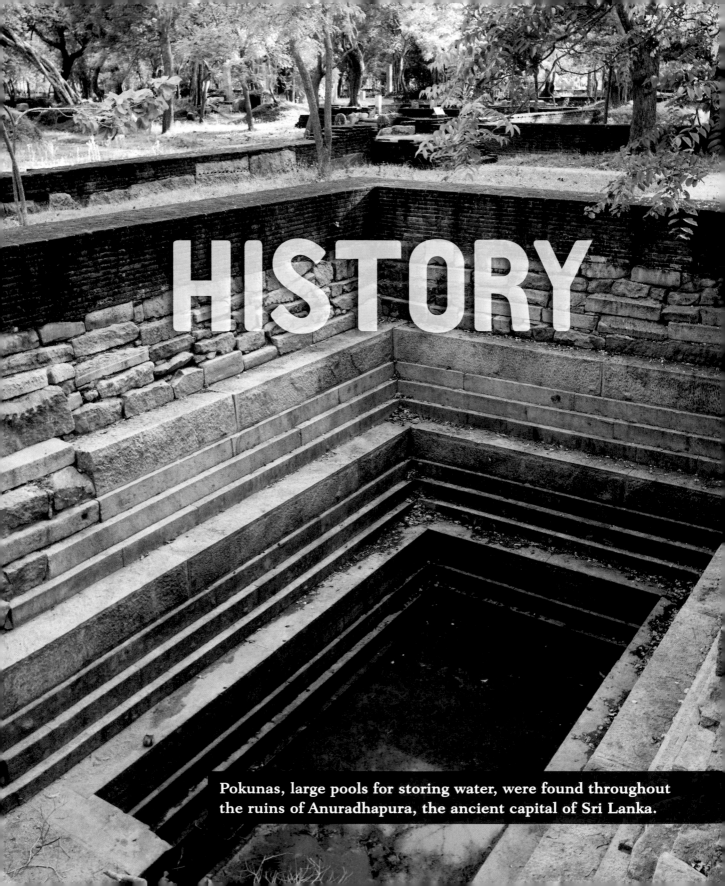

HISTORY

Pokunas, large pools for storing water, were found throughout the ruins of Anuradhapura, the ancient capital of Sri Lanka.

MYTH AND LEGEND ARE WOVEN into Sri Lanka's history, which spans 25 centuries. The *Mahavamsa* (MAH-hah-VUM-seh), a chronicle dating back to the sixth century A.D., and its sequel, the *Culavamsa* (CHOO-lah-VUM-seh), relate Sri Lanka's early history.

According to the *Mahavamsa*, before the sixth century B.C. there existed two tribes, the Yaka and Naga. Stone objects have been found that indicate that Homo sapiens probably lived in Sri Lanka around 500,000 B.C. From 5,000 B.C. until about 500 B.C., a people called Balangoda practiced stone-working technology. They dwindled with the arrival of the first settlers from India.

THE SINHALESE ARRIVE

The first royal dynasty was established by Prince Vijaya (543—505 B.C.). This Indian prince was banished from his father's North Indian kingdom because of his bullying ways. His father, Sinhabahu, was believed to be the offspring of a lion, or *sinha* (SING-hah), and a princess; hence the name Sinha, or Sinhalese, for Vijaya's descendants in Sri Lanka.

Vijaya arrived on the northeastern coast of Sri Lanka. Legend has it that a witch, Kuveni, fell in love with him. Abandoning her people, she gave up her realm to the newcomer, but after they had two children, Vijaya decided to start a blue-blooded dynasty. He ordered Kuveni and their children into the wilderness and married a South Indian princess.

His dynastic dreams, however, did not come true. It was a nephew arriving later who established the Sinhalese community in Sri Lanka.

Although Kuveni was slain by her people, her two children by Vijaya survived and are believed to be the ancestors of the aboriginal dwellers of Sri Lanka, the Veddhas.

BUDDHIST FOUNDATIONS

Culturally and spiritually, Sri Lanka has been heavily influenced by neighboring India. Buddhism was brought to the island by Mahinda, son of the great Mauryan emperor Asoka in the third century B.C. This was during the reign of Devanampiya Tissa, whose capital was at Anuradhapura.

When Buddhism became the state religion of Sri Lanka and the foundation of Sinhalese civilization, the country's classical era began. During this period, between 200 B.C. and A.D. 1200, art, architecture, and stone sculpture flourished. Huge temples were built to house the relics of the Buddha. These

Ancient wall paintings found in Mulgirigala Temple.

temples are venerated even today and never fail to inspire the beholder with their simple form, peaceful appearance, and majestic size.

Sri Lanka's ancient civilization emerged in the island's dry zone—the extensive north-central plains and a smaller area in the southeast. The legacy of this ancient past lives on in the exquisitely carved statues, temples, reservoirs, and channels in these areas. An ingenious tank for storing water covering 7 square miles (18 square km) was built by King Mahasena (A.D. 274—302). Some 200 years later, King Datusena (A.D. 460—478) built the Kalawewa (*wewa*, pronounced WAI-weh, means "tank"), a reservoir covering 7 square miles with a dam 36—58 feet (11—18 m) high and stretching 3 miles (5 km).

ANURADHAPURA: SEAT OF KINGS

Founded in the sixth century B.C., Anuradhapura is one of Sri Lanka's major historical sites. Once the seat of kings, Anuradhapura was the first capital of Sri Lanka. The city reached the height of power in the ninth century A.D., but was later displaced by Polonnaruwa.

Ruins at Anuradhapura.

In the second century B.C., Anuradhapura was the capital from which a just Tamil king named Elara ruled northern Sri Lanka. Ruhuna, the southeastern part of the island, was ruled by a Sinhalese king named Kakavan Tissa, and the southwestern region was the domain of King Kelani Tissa.

After Kelani Tissa killed a Buddhist monk, his daughter, Viharamaha Devi, was sent out to sea in a boat as a sacrifice. But winds blew the boat to a port in Ruhuna. There Kakavan Tissa married the princess and they had two sons. The elder son, Gamini, raised an army to fight Elara. He killed Elara and became known as Dutu Gemunu, or Fearless Gamini. From Anuradhapura, he ruled a now-unified country that grew in prosperity. Dutu Gemunu built many temples, the most famous being the Ruwanvelisaya, which is surrounded by a wall of stone elephants.

SIGIRIYA

Kasyapa, the eldest son of King Datusena of Anuradhapura, is even today revered by Sri Lankans. Kasyapa was afraid that his half-brother, Mogallan,

An aerial view of the ruins at Sigiriya.

would inherit the throne. So he killed his father by walling him into a corner of the Kalawewa, the tank Datusena had built. Seizing the throne, Kasyapa built a palace fortress on Sigiriya, a tall plateau-like rock, to protect himself from the wrath of the rightful heir. Kasyapa ruled from Sigiriya for 18 years, from A.D. 477 to 95. Then Mogallan attacked, and Kasyapa killed himself, mistakenly thinking he had no defense.

Halfway up Sigiriya's sheer rock face are wonderful frescoes, paintings of beautiful women, some holding lotus flowers. Beside the rock-hewn steps winding up to the palace fortress is a remarkable lime-coated wall with a mirrored surface to protect the climber moving along the steps. Sigiriya's mirrored wall carries graffiti written by visitors who praise or ridicule the bare-bosomed beauties in the frescoes.

POLONNARUWA

The capital of the kingdom was moved from Anuradhapura to Polonnaruwa in the 12th century. King Parakrama Bahu I (A.D. 1153—56), a Sinhalese king,

The capital of the kingdom was moved from Anuradhapura to Polonnaruwa.

Centuries before the birth of Christ, the island, now known as Sri Lanka, was called Thambapanni. In the Mahavamsa, *it is written that "When those who were commanded by Vijaya landed from their ship, they wearied, resting their hands on the ground. And since their hands were reddened by touching the dust of the red earth, that region and also the island was named Thambapanni (copper-colored earth)."*

The Greeks and Romans knew the island as Taprobane, a variation on Thambapanni, and the name is mentioned in several Greco-Roman texts. Ptolemy's second-century map of the island, captioned "Tabyla Asia XII," uses this name for the island he traced. The ancient Sinhalese called their homeland Heladiva (Sinhadvipa in Sanskrit; Siholadipa in Pali). Heladiva was one of the richest places in Asia, located on the main trade route linking the Middle East with Southeast Asia and China. Arab traders called Heladiva "Serendip." The English writer, Horace Walpole coined the English word serendipity *from this name.*

The first Europeans to establish permanent trading bases were the Portuguese. They colonized the island in the early 16th century and called it Ceiloa. The Dutch wrested trading rights from the Portuguese and colonized the island in the mid-17th century, changing the name to Ceylan or Zeiland. The British, who conquered the island and added it as another jewel to the British Crown in the early 19th century, changed the name to Ceylon. This was the name the island went by even after independence from the British. In 1972, when the country assumed the status of a republic, it became Sri Lanka, which means "resplendent isle."

managed to gain control of nearly the entire island. During his short reign, several Buddhist shrines and monuments were added to Polonnaruwa. King Parakrama Bahu I is best remembered for the reservoir he constructed, called Parakrama Samudra (meaning "Sea of Parakrama"), of which he said, "Let not a drop of water flow into the sea before it is used in the service of man."

THE KANDYAN KINGDOM

With the decline of the classical age, the capital was moved several times, until the last kings located their capital in Kandy. This remained the capital until 1815, when British rule began.

EUROPEAN COLONIZATION

THE PORTUGUESE The first Portuguese visit was "serendipitous." In 1505 a fleet commanded by Lourenco de Almeida was blown into the Colombo harbor and given a friendly reception by the Sinhalese king of Kotte. Impressed by the island's commercial and strategic value, the Portuguese landed in force in 1518. They were permitted to build a fort in Colombo and were given trading concessions. Soon they expanded their influence and turned from trading to ruling.

The fort at Galle was originally built by the Portuguese but was expanded by the Dutch in 1667.

With intense zeal, Portuguese missionaries converted the indigenous people to Catholicism and forbade Buddhism. They lacked an understanding of traditional Sinhalese society and were cruel in their demands. No wonder that when the Dutch appeared on the horizon as traders, the Sinhalese welcomed them as liberators.

THE DUTCH In a period of intrigue and shifting alliances in the Dutch—Portuguese—Sinhalese triumvirate, local kings and lesser officials had a greater say in the politics of the island. By 1658 the Dutch had seized the Portuguese fort in Colombo and taken hold of their last strongholds—Mannar and Jaffna in the north.

Although the Dutch East India Company was first set up in the coastal regions, its influence eventually spread inland. But the Kandyan kingdom remained intact in the central hills and eastern province.

The Dutch left a legacy in Sri Lanka in the form of printing technology, the judicial system of Roman—Dutch law, and canals radiating from Colombo. Some of these canals are still navigable by boat and one of the canals takes tourists to a bird sanctuary.

THE BRITISH The British East India Company established trading posts in Sri Lanka around 1796. Contacting the king of Kandy, the British offered to replace the Dutch as protectors of the kingdom. The Kandyans were suspicious. In typical colonizing style, the British decided to unify the island under their rule. Sensing disunity in the Kandyan court, the British sought to exploit the differences and encouraged intrigue. Eventually they captured the king of Kandy and deported him to South India. By 1815 the British ruled the entire island.

The British introduced coffee in Sri Lanka as a cash crop. Coffee exports were very successful from 1830 to 1870, replacing the former main export crop, cinnamon. In 1870, however, disease destroyed coffee plantations in Sri Lanka. Tea and rubber replaced coffee and became better cash-earners.

Evidence of Sri Lanka's colonial past can be seen through the British coat of arms placed above the entrance to the Dutch fort.

Together with cash crops, the British introduced cheap labor from South India. Initially South Indian Tamils working on coffee plantations would return to India after the harvests. However, tea and rubber required year-round care, so Tamil laborers began to settle in Sri Lanka, forming a new group of Sri Lankan Tamils—Indian Tamils, who were distinct from the long-established Jaffna Tamils.

The British built roads and railroads in Sri Lanka and developed trade and commerce in both urban and plantation areas. The villagers, however, were mostly neglected. Their lands were purchased for a small sum to extend the tea estates, and they survived by growing food on whatever land they could find.

Kotte was the seat of kings from the mid-14th to the 16th century. The Sinhalese expression "Like the Portuguese who went to Kotte" describes how the first Portuguese envoy was led by a circuitous route from Colombo to Kotte, so he would not realize that Kotte was only 5 miles (8 km) away. The ploy worked.

A few years later, a second Portuguese envoy, General Payoe de Souza, arrived and met King Parakramabahu VIII. His visit had a different ending. By 1557 the Portuguese had allied themselves with the next Kotte king, then killed him, baptized another Sri Lankan king, and moved him to Colombo, and finally destroyed Kotte.

The British ruled Sri Lanka from 1815 to 1948. A governor-general in Colombo, government agents, and other officials administered the nine provinces into which the island was divided.

NATIONALISM AND INDEPENDENCE

From the late 19th century, a growing national political consciousness in Sri Lanka created a call for constitutional reform and self-government. Although independence was still a long way off, in 1931 the British gave the right to vote to Sri Lankan men and women over 21 years old. (At the time, this was certainly progress; in Britain, women got the right to vote only in 1929.)

When World War II broke out, Sri Lankan leaders suspended their nationalistic struggles and pledged support for the war effort. Trincomalee and Colombo became important link ports for Allied warships. A couple of Japanese war planes arrived on Easter Sunday in 1942, probably to study the terrain and plan an attack. They were repulsed.

Ceylon was the headquarters of the South East Asia Command (SEAC) under the charismatic Lord Louis Mountbatten, the last viceroy of India and later the favorite uncle of Prince Charles, the current heir to the British throne. Trincomalee in northeastern Ceylon was an important harbor for the Allied navy.

In 1945 Sri Lankans resumed their agitation for independence. Although they were granted internal self-government, with the British retaining control of defense and foreign policy, nothing short of full independence would satisfy them. Finally the Ceylon Independence Act of 1947 conferred dominion status on the country. A year later, on February 4, Sri Lanka celebrated its independence from colonial rule with fireworks, feasting, and jubilation.

SHIFTS OF POWER

The ceremonial opening of Sri Lanka's first parliament session six days after its independence from Britain.

In the years before and just after independence, the spirit of nationalism ran high. Everyone was a Sri Lankan first; and a Sinhalese, Tamil, Muslim, or a Burgher next. But trouble soon followed, leading to the election of six governments in less than 35 years. Even today Sri Lankan politics is irretrievably tied to economic troubles and ethnic tension.

Don Stephen Senanayake (1884—1952) was Sri Lanka's first prime minister. The failure of his United National Party (UNP) to maintain a strong economy led to its downfall. In 1956 a new opposition party, the Sri Lanka Freedom Party (SLFP), led by S.W.R.D. Bandaranaike (1899—1959) and backed by Buddhist leaders, won the national election. However, the party was divided on many issues, and tensions led to the prime minister's assassination in 1959.

The UNP took over the following year, but it was so weak that elections were held again just four months later. Sirimavo Bandaranaike, the assassinated prime minister's widow, led the SLFP to victory. She addressed the country's ethnic and economic issues, but the issue of making Sinhala the

Known popularly as the Tamil Tigers, the Liberation Tigers of Tamil Eelam (the LTTE) was a separatist militant organization based in northern Sri Lanka. Founded in 1976 by Velupillai Prabhakaran, it waged a violent campaign to create an independent state in the north and east of Sri Lanka for the Tamils. This campaign developed into a civil war that started in 1983 and only ended after the military defeat of the LTTE by the Sri Lankan Army in 2009.

At the height of its strength in 2002, the LTTE numbered at least 10,000 fighters and controlled an area of approximately 5,792 square miles (15,000 square km), running a virtual independent mini-state. The LTTE carried out numerous attacks, suicide bombings, and atrocities over the course of the war, and were branded as terrorists by much of the international community. After the breakdown of the peace process in 2006, the Sri Lankan military launched an offensive that brought the entire country under their control by 2009. Prabhakaran was killed in May 2009 and Sri Lankan President Mahinda Rajapaksa declared victory over the LTTE.

national language proved so unpopular among the Burghers and the Tamils that Bandaranaike lost the 1965 elections.

The UNP returned to power, promoting agricultural production, but unemployment rose. Bandaranaike won the 1970 elections to lead a coalition government, the United Front. The next year, reforms gave the state control of the economy and a new constitution. The Dominion of Ceylon became the Republic of Sri Lanka in 1972. Unfortunately the reforms alienated the Tamil minority, in particular the educated unemployed, who demanded the creation of an independent Tamil state, Eelam.

The "united front" was falling apart, and in the 1977 elections, the UNP once again sailed into power, led by Junius Richard Jayewardene (1906–1996). In 1978 the constitution was amended again. The country was renamed the Democratic Socialist Republic of Sri Lanka, and a presidential system of government was introduced, with the president serving as both head of state and head of the government. Jayewardene reversed government policies, promoting free enterprise and liberalizing the economy. Foreign investment

Along with other national leaders of Sinhalese, Tamil, Muslim, and Burgher heritage, Don Stephen Senanayake, affectionately called "the Father of the Nation," led the constitutional reform movement that gave Sri Lanka independence from the British.

Serving as the minister of agriculture and lands (1931—47), Senanayake engineered the rebirth of irrigation development in the country's dry zone. As Sri Lanka's first prime minister (1947—52), with Lord Soulbury as governor-general, Senanayake's moderate policies steered the country along the path of nation rebuilding. His special area of interest was self-sufficiency in food production.

Senanayake died in 1952 while his United National Party was still in power. His son Dudley succeeded him as Sri Lanka's prime minister.

was promoted, and the economy grew. The Jayewardene government was re-elected in 1982.

MODERN HISTORY

In mid-1983 Tamil guerrillas, demanding an independent state, began a campaign of terrorist attacks. The Sinhalese retaliated, rioting against the Tamils. This marked the beginning of a long period of ethnic strife that developed into a full-blown civil war, causing the peoples of the east and northeast much hardship. The civil war only came to a close in 2009, when the Liberation Tigers of Tamil Eelam (LTTE), known more popularly as the Tamil Tigers, was defeated by government forces.

In 1988 Jayewardene retired and Ranasinghe Premadasa became president. In 1993 Premadasa was assassinated. His successor, D. B. Wijetunga, called for elections the next year, when the People's Alliance (PA) came to power, with Chandrika Kumaratunga as prime minister. Kumaratunga soon became Sri Lanka's first woman president, following in the footsteps of her mother, Sirimavo, who was the world's first woman prime minister.

After seven years in power, the PA lost ground. In the 2001 elections, the main opponent, the UNP, won just five seats short of a majority in the parliament, with the country now falling under the joint leadership of Kumaratunga and the UNP's Ranil Wickremesinghe. In the parliamentary elections in 2004, a new grouping, the United People's Freedom Alliance, gained a slim majority in parliament and the alliance's leader Mahinda Rajapaksa was sworn in as Sri Lanka's 13th prime minister in April 2004.

In the presidential elections in November 2005, Mahinda Rajapaksa was nominated as the SLFP candidate and former prime minister Ranil Wickremesinghe was the UNP candidate. The election was held on November 17, 2005, and Mahinda Rajapaksa was elected the fifth president of Sri Lanka with 50.29 percent of the votes. Wickremesinghe came in a close second with 48.43 percent. Ratnasiri Wickremanayake was appointed the 22nd prime minister on November 21, 2005, to fill the post vacated by Rajapaksa. President Rajapraksa won re-election in the last presidential elections in 2010.

INTERNET LINKS

http://infolanka.com/org/srilanka/hist.html

This site offers numerous links to many fascinating aspects of Sri Lankan history, art, religion, and people.

www.explorelanka.com/places/nc/anu.htm

This website is a guide to the ancient ruins of Sri Lanka's most famous Buddhist kingdom, with coverage of temples, statues, history, and mythology.

www.srilankaguardian.org/2011/02/63rd-independence-from-britain-photos.html

This site includes photos with captions of Sri Lanka's most recent Independence Day celebration from a leading Sri Lankan newspaper.

GOVERNMENT

City Hall in Colombo.

3

FOLLOWING INDEPENDENCE IN 1948 Sri Lanka opted to remain within the Commonwealth of Nations as a free and sovereign state. In 1974 it became a republic, still within the Commonwealth.

In 1978 a new constitution with a French-style presidential system of government was adopted. Sri Lanka has enjoyed democracy with universal suffrage since 1931. Politics today in Sri Lanka is controlled by rival coalitions led by the left-wing Sri Lanka Freedom Party (SLFP), headed by President Mahinda Rajapaksa, and the more right-wing United National Party (UNP), led by former prime minister Ranil Wickremesinghe.

The inauguration of the Sri Lankan parliament in 2010.

The president of the Democratic Socialist Republic of Sri Lanka is head of state, chief executive, and supreme commander of the armed forces. He or she is elected by the people for a term of six years. The president appoints the prime minister, members of the cabinet, and court judges. He or she has the power to dissolve the parliament and call for a national referendum.

The president heads the executive branch of the government; the parliament holds legislative power. The judicial branch consists of the Supreme Court and a court of appeals.

PARLIAMENT AND PROVINCES

Sri Lanka's legislative body is a unicameral, or single-house, parliament consisting of 225 members who are elected at the constituency or district level for a period of six years.

Sri Lanka's president Mahinda Rajapaksa, speaking during the 66th annual United Nations General Assembly.

The Ministry of Provincial Councils and Local Government oversees nine provincial councils, whose members are elected for six-year terms. The president appoints provincial governors from outside the councils; ministers are selected from the pool of elected councilors. The provincial councils work with a network of district councils. Municipal councils in the cities and urban councils in the towns answer to their respective provincial councils.

In 1987 the government agreed to give greater authority to the provinces. The provincial councils exercise their influence in areas such as rural development, education, health, and social services.

ELECTIONS

There are more than 12 million eligible voters in Sri Lanka and an abundance of newspapers in the three main languages—Sinhala, Tamil, and English—that reach even remote villages. Radio, television, and the Internet also bring news to the people nationwide.

Sri Lankan voters line up outside a polling station in Colombo.

In the most recent presidential elections, Mahinda Rajapaksa of the United People's Freedom Alliance was elected for a six-year term for the first time in November 2005, defeating former prime minister Ranil Wickramasinghe, the United National Party candidate. The constitution of Sri Lanka allows the president to ask for a fresh election after four years into his first term of office, and Rajapaksa announced his intention to hold fresh elections in late 2009. In the presidential elections of January 2010, President Rajapaksa was re-elected after winning more than 6 million votes, or 57.88 percent. He was closely followed by his New Democratic Front rival, former general Sarath Fonseka, who won 40.15 percent of the votes. The Sri Lanka Freedom Party currently holds 102 seats in the parliament, followed by the United National Party, with 43 seats.

This was the sixth presidential election in Sri Lanka since the formulation of the new constitution in 1978. Sri Lankans take their duty to vote very seriously. When the fiercely nationalistic Sinhalese JVP party attempted a boycott of the 1989—90 presidential and parliamentary elections through a terror campaign, threatening to kill the first seven voters at each polling booth, Sri Lankans still went to the polls to cast their ballots, no doubt trembling with fear. Even the 2001 elections—one of the country's most violent—saw a high voter turnout. Around 50 deaths were reported during the election campaign, and the army and police were deployed to ensure peace on polling day.

POLITICAL PARTIES

Sri Lanka has a two-party system where two political parties dominate the political landscape. In recent decades the United National Party and the Sri Lanka Freedom Party have been the largest parties. Political parties in Sri Lanka range from the democratic to the radical. The major ones include the following:

SRI LANKA FREEDOM PARTY (SLFP)   S.W.R.D. Bandaranaike formed this breakaway party when he crossed over from the UNP to the opposition in the early 1950s. In 1956 the SLFP won a landslide victory, and Bandaranaike became the prime minister. He was assassinated in 1959 and was succeeded by his widow, Sirimavo Bandaranaike, the world's first woman prime minister. The SLFP has won the last two elections under the leadership of Mahinda Rajapaksa.

UNITED NATIONAL PARTY (UNP) D. S. Senanayake, independent Sri Lanka's first prime minister, led the UNP from its formation in 1946. The party won a major victory in 2001, and its leader Ranil Wickremesinghe was sworn in as the country's newest prime minister. However, in elections in 2005 and 2010, the party finished second to the Sri Lanka Freedom Party.

LANKA SAMA SAMAJA PARTY (LSSP)   Formed in 1935, the LSSP is one of the oldest political parties. It was in the forefront of the struggle for independence and joined a coalition government for a couple of years in the 1960s; it has lost much of its clout now, and holds just two seats in the current parliament.

As the president of Sri Lanka (1988—93), Ranasinghe Premadasa embarked on a far-reaching program of economic and industrial development. In order to integrate the economy with the international market, trade policies were liberalized. Export-oriented industries were promoted in order to bring more foreign exchange into the country. Foreign investors were encouraged to set up industries in tax-free zones. In 1992 a "decade of exports" was declared, and geographic limits on tax-free zones were removed when the whole country was declared a tax-free Export Processing Zone (EPZ). State enterprises were privatized, and workers became stockholders in these companies. Almost 10,000 employees from 23 privatized companies received free stock. Great efforts were made to promote employment. In 1992 Premadasa encouraged a project to establish 200 garment factories in rural areas, each providing 500 jobs.

While many government subsidies for the poor and the unemployed were withdrawn, Premadasa's Janasaviya, or People's Power program, ensured that the poorest of the poor were given money to support themselves and start income-generating businesses. His other projects included the Gam Udawa, or Village Awakening, which set up a massive trade fair in remote areas and developed these areas, and the Million Houses Project. Premadasa was assassinated by an LTTE suicide bomber on May 1, 1993, as he was going to the May Day rally. He was succeeded by D. B. Wijetunge, who had served as prime minister.

Never in Sri Lanka had a leader risen to power with so much mass appeal—not counting the father of the nation, D. S. Senanayake—and been so unsuccessful in steering the country to peace and prosperity than Chandrika Bandaranaike Kumaratunga, president from 1994 to 2005. She has been Sri Lanka's only female president to date.

Kumaratunga is the second daughter of the late S.W.R.D. Bandaranaike— a former prime minister himself—and Sirimavo Bandaranaike—the world's first woman prime minister. Her actor-turned-politician husband, Wijaya Kumaratunga, met with the same fate as her father—he too was assassinated. An LTTE suicide bomber nearly killed Chandrika Kumaratunga as well after a public meeting close to election day in 2000; she was blinded in one eye.

Chandrika Kumaratunga led the PA coalition to success in 1994, winning a record 62 percent of the votes. She won the presidential elections again in 2000, beating the chief opposition candidate, UNP's Ranil Wickremasinghe, the standing prime minister. However, the ongoing civil war, an economic downturn, and corruption within her government hurt Kumaratunga's popularity.

COMMUNIST PARTY (CP) Formed in 1943, this leftist party is part of the PA coalition. Its chairman for more than 40 years, Pieter Keuneman, died in 1997. Its current leader is D.E.W. Gunasekera.

THE SRI LANKA MUSLIM CONGRESS was formed to protect the interests of Muslims in the Eastern province. The party holds eight seats in the current parliament.

JANATA VIMUKTI PERAMUNA (JVP) This Sinhalese rebel party terrorized the country and brought near anarchy under the leadership of its founder, Rohana Wijeweera, in 1971 and again in 1988. In 1989 the army executed Wijeweera. The party went underground until 1994 when it resurfaced and entered mainstream politics. In the 2010 elections, four of its members were elected to parliament.

LIBERATION TIGERS OF TAMIL EELAM (LTTE) Known the world over as a terrorist party, the LTTE fought the government's armed forces from 1983 in an attempt to set up a separate Tamil state, called Eelam, in the north. The government outlawed the party in 1998, after a bombing in which 16 people were killed at a sacred 16th-century Buddhist shrine. In 2010 a ceasefire was declared and a peace agreement put in place.

UNITED PEOPLE'S FREEDOM ALLIANCE This new political grouping was formed as recently as 2003 as a broad alliance of the old Sri Lanka Freedom Party and other left-wing and Muslim parties under the leadership of Mahinda Rajapaksa. This alliance dominates the current parliament, with 162 seats.

INTERNET LINKS

http://news.bbc.co.uk/1/hi/world/south_asia/3602101.stm

This BBC article offers a concise profile of President Rajapaksa before the 2010 elections.

www.mahindarajapaksa.com/

The current president's personal website offers links to the president's various projects.

www.priu.gov.lk/

This is the official site of the Sri Lankan government, with hundreds of links to news stories, photographs, and data.

www.serconoline.com/promos/sep/fnst/images/sri_b.jpg

This map shows Sri Lanka's nine provinces and provincial capitals.

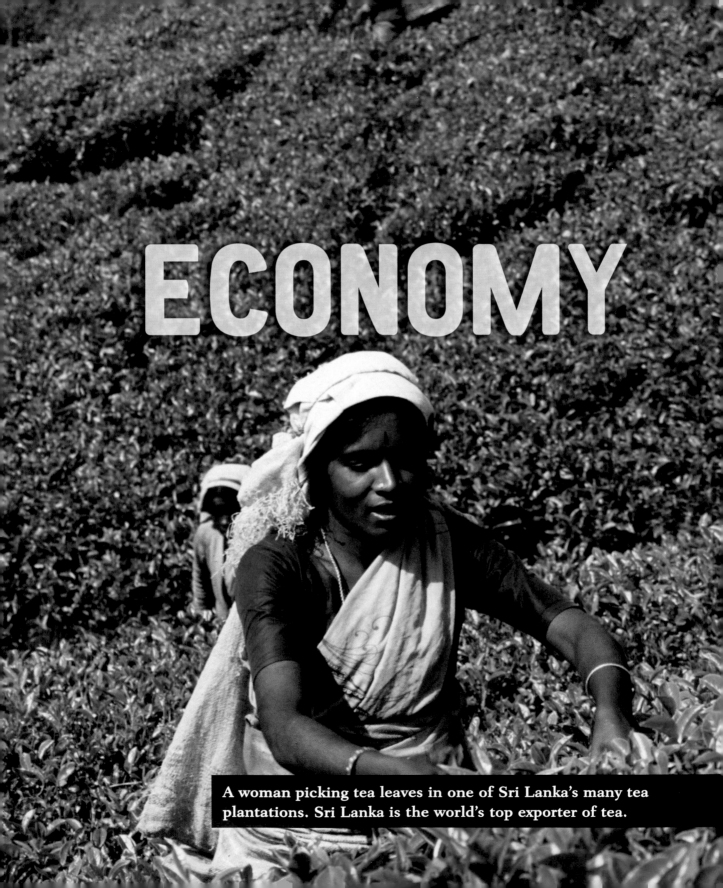

ECONOMY

A woman picking tea leaves in one of Sri Lanka's many tea plantations. Sri Lanka is the world's top exporter of tea.

4

S RI LANKA TRADITIONALLY HAS an agriculture-based economy, producing rice, rubber, tea, coconut, and many other plantation crops.

Since the 1980s, however, industrial growth has made the manufacturing sector an important contributor to the Sri Lankan economy. Tourism is also a vital source of foreign exchange earnings. Other sources of revenue are wages sent home by migrant workers and earnings from the export of manufactured garments and precious and semiprecious stones.

DIVERSIFICATION AND GROWTH

In 1977 the Jayewardene government implemented a growth policy that encouraged private enterprise in different sectors of the economy and

Sri Lanka has benefited from strong economic growth in recent years, especially since a ceasefire was made with the Tamil Tigers in 2010.

A worker undergoing training to install electrical switchboards.

promoted the growth of industry. This broadened the range of exports to include manufactured petroleum products, garments, gems, nontraditional commodities such as leather and rubber goods, minerals, and even cut flowers and ornamental fish.

Between 1978 and 1983 economists pointed to Sri Lanka as an economic model. Growing at a rate of more than 8 percent per year, the Sri Lankan economy outpaced even developed countries. But the boom period ended when ethnic clashes broke out in 1983 between the Sinhalese and the Tamils. Growth fell to 2.7 percent by 1988, and then rose in 1990 to 6.2 percent, showing signs of another boom. But a downward trend followed instead, starting at 4.3 percent in 1992 and sliding to less than 1 percent in 2001. In 2001 Sri Lanka faced bankruptcy, with a huge government debt. The impending currency crisis was avoided after a ceasefire was made with the LTTE and loans were made available by international investors.

The global financial crisis of 2008—2009 put Sri Lanka's public finances under extreme pressure, but an IMF (International Monetary Fund) loan following the end of the civil war in 2010 has restored international confidence. The Sri Lankan economy grew by a healthy 6—7 percent in 2006—2008, and still managed to grow by 3.8 percent in 2009, despite the global recession. The economy was estimated to have expanded further to over 9 percent in 2010, and looks like it will continue this healthy growth with the end of hostilities.

An employee learning about metal processing. The Sri Lankan government has been making efforts to diversify its economy.

INDUSTRY AND FOREIGN INVESTMENT

Sri Lanka's manufacturing sector has made great strides in the past three decades. The textile and garment industry has been a star performer, while

Garment workers sewing items for British retailer Marks and Spencers. Many foreign garment and textile companies have production factories in Sri Lanka.

food processing and chemicals have also risen in importance. There are approximately 900 clothing factories in Sri Lanka providing garments for the world's leading fashion designing labels, like Victoria's Secret, Liz Claiborne, and Tommy Hilfiger. The government has looked to foreign investors to develop local industries. Companies pay lower taxes or no taxes and enjoy duty-free imports for investments in selected industries, such as electronics.

The government has made efforts to build the country's infrastructure to attract foreign investment. There are 12 EPZs (export processing zones) with paved roads, reliable power and water supplies, security systems, telecommunications, post offices, shipping agents, banking and customs services, medical clinics, and recreational facilities.

The civil war was a threat to foreign investment. In 2001 Tamil Tigers attacked the air force base and international airport at Katunayake, destroying 10 aircraft and killing four air force personnel. Some foreign investors reacted by pulling out, and many factory workers lost their jobs.

However, following the end of the war in 2009, Sri Lanka has undergone wholesale reconstruction, including extensive rebuilding of its rail and road network.

AGRICULTURE

Sri Lanka is primarily an agricultural society, with a history of growing rice and grain stretching back 2,500 years. More than 30 percent of the population works on small farms. Commercial crops accounted for over 90 percent of exports in 1970, but the figure had fallen below 20 percent by 1997. By 2010, however, agriculture made up less than 13 percent of gross domestic product. Sri Lanka's agricultural exports include tea, rubber, coconut, cocoa, coffee, tobacco, and spices such as pepper, cinnamon, cardamom, cloves, and nutmeg. Rice, fruit, and vegetables are grown for local consumption.

The vast irrigation network of the Mahaweli Diversion Project has made diversification of Sri Lankan agriculture possible. This ambitious project has resulted in the construction of five dams at strategic points across the longest river in Sri Lanka. Cultivating chilies, onions, and vegetables such

The Sri Lankan agricultural sector has benefited from irrigation channels like this.

Women transplanting rice. Rice cultivation is labor-intensive and backbreaking work.

as cucumbers and baby corn has made some Mahaweli settlers rich, while imports of rice, lentils, and potatoes have fallen drastically. The water from the dams has also been used to produce hydroelectricity.

Meanwhile *chena* (CHAIN-neh), the slash-and-burn farming method, continues with disastrous results for virgin forests. This farming method involves the farmer cutting and clearing an area of a forest, before setting fire to it just before the onset of rains. Following the rains, the ground is cultivated with crops of cereals and vegetables. The harvest is completed soon after the rainy season, leaving the ground fallow until the following season. After about five years of this style of cultivation, the land becomes unproductive and a new patch is cleared. The government and environmental groups hope that the Mahaweli project will encourage more farmers to cultivate fixed plots of land, rather than shift from place to place.

TEA

Tea has been a crucial part of the Sri Lankan economy since colonial times, and a top foreign exchange earner, with tea contributing up to 15 percent of

HOW TO MAKE A GREAT CUP OF CEYLON TEA

Bring the water to a boil.

Rinse the teapot and tea cups with hot water.

Put the tea leaves in a teapot.

Pour the boiling water into the pot containing the tea leaves.

Keep the lid closed while allowing the tea to brew for 4—5 minutes. To get the best taste, avoid over-brewing.

Strain the tea out into cups using a tea strainer.

Add milk and sugar to taste.

The quantity of tea leaves used will vary according to taste. Generally 0.35 ounces (10 grams) of tea makes four cups.

the annual gross domestic product. In 1995 Sri Lanka became the world's largest exporter of tea in the modern era, a position it still holds today. Sri Lankan tea is exported all over the world, with Russia, the Middle East, and Europe being the chief destinations. Sri Lankan tea production rose to a record 702.1 million pounds (318.47 million kilograms) in 2008.

Until the 1860s coffee was Ceylon's main cash crop, but a coffee fungus killed off many of the coffee plantations and forced the estate owners to diversify into other crops. In 1867 James Taylor, a British tea planter, established the island's first tea plantation on the Loolecondera estate in Kandy. The first shipment of Ceylon tea, a consignment of just 23 pounds (10 kg), was sent to London in 1873; and by 1899, 400,000 acres (161,874 hectares) of land were being used for tea growing. By the 1960s the total tea production and exports were more than 220,462 tons (200,000 metric tons), and by 1965 Sri Lanka became the world's largest tea exporter for the first time. In the early 1970s the tea estates owned by British companies were nationalized by the government, which introduced land reforms so that no single farmer was allowed to own more than 50 acres (20.2 ha).

The tea is grown in the central highlands, where high rainfall, low temperatures, and constant humidity provide ideal conditions for producing high-quality tea. Over 853 square miles (2,209 square km), or approximately 4 percent of the country's land area, is covered with tea plantations. There are six main tea-producing areas: Galle, in the south; Ratnapura, about 55 miles (88.5 km) east of the capital Colombo; Kandy, the low region near the ancient royal capital; Nuwara Eliya, the highest area that produces the finest teas; Dimbula, west of the central mountains; and Uva, located east of Dimbula.

Stilt fishermen in Koggala.

The tea sector employs, directly or indirectly, more than a million Sri Lankans. Most of the workers are female, some as young as 12 years, the minimum working age in Sri Lanka. The workers usually live on the estate where they work, and their whole lives revolve around the life of the estate. Sri Lanka is one of the few countries where each tea leaf is picked by hand rather than by a machine. If machinery were used, coarse leaves and twigs might be mixed in, therefore reducing the quality of the final product. Experienced tea pickers can harvest up to 40 pounds (25 kg) of leaves per day.

The finished tea is divided into grades and types, including the high-grade Ceylon black tea, the nutty-flavored Ceylon green tea, and the delicate (and expensive) Ceylon white, or "silver tips," tea.

FISH, FLESH, AND FOWL

The fishing season is controlled by the monsoons. Fishermen stay on the southwestern beaches during the northeast monsoon and move to the northeastern coast during the southwest monsoon. Several inland fisheries have been set up with Japanese aid. The 2004 tsunami had a very damaging effect on fishing activity in Sri Lanka, but the industry has since recovered with the massive rebuilding of the infrastructure. Fishing yields in the north of the island increased markedly after the end of the civil war in 2009.

THE TEXTURE OF COCO-NUTTERY

It is almost impossible for a visitor to leave Sri Lanka without seeing a coconut palm. Sri Lankans owe much of their lifestyle to the leaves, fruit, and even flowers of the coconut palm, which they call the "tree of life."

The flowers are used for decorative purposes at ceremonies. An oil lamp is placed in the inflorescence in a clay pot.

The leaves are often used in floral decorations. The creamy and supple young leaves can be trimmed, rolled, and folded into pretty shapes. The leaves of the coconut palm do have more essential uses, however, such as providing thatching for roofs. A bunch of mature leaf stalks, with their blades shaved off, makes an excellent broom when secured at the thicker end with a cord. The thicker part of the stalk, shaved clean and smooth and sharpened at one end, makes an excellent barbecue skewer. The leaves can also be braided into fans and screening mats.

The nuts are by far the most important part of the coconut palm, being both food and a cash crop. The coir—the thick, rough, fibrous outside layer—is woven into floor mats, tiles, or rope. The hard brown shell underneath the coir, when halved, may be used as a bowl for food or a large spoon or a container for collecting latex from rubber trees (another cash crop). The thick white kernel inside the shell is delicious: soft and slippery when young, hard and crunchy when mature. The latter is grated and squeezed for milk, which is added to curries, rice, and pancakes or made into desserts. Grated rather than dehydrated coconut forms the rich base of candy and other rich Sri Lankan sweets. The dried kernel, called copra, yields oil when pressed. Finally in the hollow shell is the coconut water, a clear, sweet, thirst-quenching drink.

The sap of the coconut palm is used to make thelijja (TEL-lee-jah), a nonalcoholic drink, or toddy. A tapper extracts the sap, which is then fermented for a few hours.

Borrowed from Edward Lear, writer and artist

The unskilled in Sri Lanka have few options when it comes to earning a living. Some live just outside Colombo in shanty towns and do casual labor, such as loading and cleaning, in the commercial district. Those in the rural areas sell fruit and other food items on the streets. Many unemployed Sri Lankans register at agencies to find work as housemaids, babysitters, drivers, and the like in the Middle East and other Asian countries. These individuals have to be healthy and physically fit in order to work the long hours required, often 15 to 16 hours a day. The usual contract is for two years, and this may be renewed once, several times, or after an interval, depending on the work permit rules of the foreign country.

The government encourages the unemployed to seek work opportunities abroad. There are more than a million Sri Lankans working abroad. It was estimated that in 2009, 130,000 Sri Lankan women moved abroad to work. Those with skills go to the Middle East, Australia, the United States, and Western Europe. The Bureau of Foreign Employment trains domestic workers who migrate to Asian countries and introduces them to conditions they will meet in their host countries. The bureau, with several nongovernmental organizations and trade unions, now helps returned migrants start income-generating projects at home, to avoid the social consequences of broken homes and school dropouts. Migration of women workers is discouraged for the same reason.

Cattle are more often reared for their milk and to do farm work than for their meat. They draw carts, plow fields, and help farmers thresh harvested rice stalks. Beef is eaten, but because Buddhists believe that life is precious and Hindus hold the cow sacred, the slaughter of cattle is decreasing.

Chicken runs (enclosures where chickens are raised for profit) are becoming popular; nowadays even housewives are maintaining them to supplement the family income.

TOURISM

Tourism is an important foreign exchange earner for Sri Lanka. From 192,000 in 1978, tourist arrivals to the island had reached 407,000 in 1982. However, ethnic conflict from 1983 to 2009 made it highly risky for foreigners to visit the country. After the island welcomed 400,414 visitors in 2000, the LTTE dealt another blow to tourism by attacking the airport at Katunayake in 2001. The 2004 tsunami also had a negative impact on the tourist industry. However, since the end of the war in 2009, tourism has grown, with the island receiving almost half a million visitors in 2009 and 650,000 in 2010.

Sri Lanka's big attractions are its beaches, ancient cities, wildlife, charming rural areas, and famous hospitality. Sri Lanka is home to eight UNESCO heritage sites and 15 national parks. The government is also promoting the country as a convention center, with the $3 million Bandaranaike Memorial International Conference Hall, reputedly one of the best conference complexes in South Asia.

GEMS

Among the natural treasures of Sri Lanka are precious and semiprecious gems, which have attracted traders from all over the world for centuries. Sri Lanka's gems are part of the reason the island has been called the "Jewel of the Indian Ocean." Historical records show that Sri Lankan gems have been mined and fashioned into fine jewelry for more than 2,500 years. Sri Lanka has deposits of as many as 50 of the 140 varieties of gemstones in the world. Among the best known are blue sapphires, rubies, topaz, zircons, garnets, amethysts, moonstones, quartz, and tourmaline. Today Sri Lanka has one of the fastest-growing gem-cutting and gem-finishing industries in the world. More than 30,000 skilled gem cutters are employed nationwide. The government has provided tax incentives for entrepreneurs and has established a training center for gem cutting to increase the pool of skilled workers to promote the industry.

INTERNET LINKS

www.angelfire.com/wi/SriLanka/ceyl_tea.htm#History%20of%20 Ceylon%20Tea

This website tells the story of tea production in Ceylon, with an account of its history, production, and how to make the perfect cup of tea.

www.galenfrysinger.com/rice_farming,_sri_lanka.htm

This site contains a photo essay on rice farming in Sri Lanka.

www.galenfrysinger.com/tea_growing.htm

This site includes photos and descriptions of tea production in Sri Lanka.

ENVIRONMENT

The Menik Ganga River.

5

S RI LANKA HAS A HIGH LEVEL of biological diversity due to the topography and climate of the country.

In addition many of the island's plants and animals are indigenous. Some 23 percent of flowering plants and 22 percent of mammals in Sri Lanka are unique to this island, which is a biodiversity "hotspot."

In ancient times Sri Lanka's natural environment was protected by royal decree. Following the teachings of the Buddha, all life was declared sacred, and animals lived in sanctuaries. One of the five daily precepts Buddhists continue to observe today is to avoid harming living things, including plants.

Despite its small size, Sri Lanka is one of the most biologically diverse countries in Asia.

Sri Lanka is home to beautiful beaches and lush tropical rain forests.

Large-scale destruction of Sri Lanka's flora and fauna began during colonial times. Forests were felled to make way for plantations, and animals were killed for sport or trade.

Post-independence development decimated forests to accommodate village expansion and urban sprawl. Elephants in particular suffered the loss of their natural habitat, as the jungle was converted to sugarcane plantations. Herds were displaced and, as a result, they began rampaging through cultivated land. Farmers reacted in turn by killing these noble animals in an attempt to protect their crops.

The Sri Lankan government is leading conservation efforts, and laws are in place to protect the island's wildlife. The Ministry of Environment is in charge of environmental affairs on the national level. Operating under the Ministry of Environment's wing are the Central Environmental Authority (CEA), which carries out environmental impact studies and controls air, water and soil pollution, and the Department of Forestry, which looks after the management and conservation of natural forests.

FORESTS

At the start of the 20th century, 75 percent of Sri Lanka was covered by dense forest. Large areas were cleared during the colonial years to make way for coffee, tea, and rubber plantations. Deforestation has continued to the present day, and less than 20 percent of the island remains under forest cover, mainly in the reserves. Unfortunately, over the last 20 years, Sri Lanka has had one of the highest rates of deforestation in the world. Large tracts of rain forest were cleared in the 1980s and 1990s by government soldiers as a consequence of the civil war. The Sri Lankan army and the Tamil rebels felled more than 2.5 million palmyra trees for building purposes. At the same time, many farmers were displaced by the fighting and moved to land in forested areas to establish new farms.

The kind of vegetation that grows in a particular place depends on the area's topography, climate, and soil. Sri Lanka's, with its hills and plains, monsoon seasons, and dry and wet zones, exhibits a diversity of forest

THE LION AND THE ELEPHANT

The Sinharajah forest reserve occupies an area of 34 square miles (89 square km) in the Sabaragamuwa and Southern provinces. Most of the forest was declared a reserve in 1875. In 1937 explorer John Baker described the Sinharajah *as "the only considerable patch of virgin tropical rain forest in the island."*

It remains Sri Lanka's last tropical lowland rain forest.

The history of the forest is tied in legend to the history of the Sinhalese, descendants of a mighty lion and a princess. The word sinharajah *(SING-hah-RAH-jah) means "lion king." The name may also refer to the large size of the forest or to its previous royal status as land belonging to the ancient kings. Yet another legend tells that the forest was the last refuge of the lion, which no longer exists on the island.*

In 1971 the government began a selective logging project to extract timber from the forest for a sawmill at Kosgama, 53 miles (85 km) to the northwest. Largely due to public pressure, in 1977 logging was banned in the forest. The next year the forest was declared a biosphere reserve, and in 1989, it made the UNESCO list of Natural World Heritage Sites.

The elephant orphanage at Pinnawela, a 30-minute drive from Kandy, is home to more than 80 elephants of different ages. The orphanage was set up in 1975 to care for baby elephants whose mothers had been killed or trapped in the wild. Injured and displaced elephants can also find refuge at the orphanage, and calves have been bred in captivity. Visitors to Pinnawela get to see elephant herds taking a bath in the river or baby elephants guzzling milk from gigantic feeding bottles.

types—tropical rain forests and dry-zone forests, mangrove swamps and coastal vegetation, mountain forests, scrublands, and grasslands.

The most common forest type on the island is the semi-evergreen forest, largely in the dry zone. Though these forests consist mainly of evergreen trees, they also have some deciduous trees. In the wet zone, vegetation type varies by altitude. Wet evergreen forests, or rain forests, grow both in the lowlands and in the hills. Grasslands cover a small part of the lowlands. Mangroves and marshes grow in bays on the coast, while swamps flourish in freshwater areas.

Apart from illicit felling and selective logging, developmental projects, such as colonization programs to resettle people from the congested towns to cleared jungle areas, harm the forests' chances of survival. The building of dams affects river vegetation, while aquaculture destroys mangrove swamps. Shifting, or *chena*, cultivation is one cause of the disappearance of natural vegetation in the dry areas.

ENDANGERED ANIMALS

Sri Lanka is home to 86 mammal species, including the elephant, jackal, bear, wild boar, buffalo, sambar, and the langur monkey. Of these 41 are

Elephants from the Pinnewala Elephant Orphanage enjoying a mid-afternoon bath.

classified as threatened, nine of them critically endangered, by the International Union for Conservation of Nature (IUCN). Among the most notable endangered animals are the Asian elephant, jungle shrew, Pearson's long-clawed shrew, purple-faced leaf monkey, Sri Lankan long-tailed shrew, and Sri Lankan shrew. Vulnerable animals include the dhole, dugong, Eurasian otter, fishing cat, rusty spotted cat, sloth bear, slow loris, toque macaque, and Sri Lankan giant squirrel.

A leopard stalking prey in Yala West National Park.

The elephant population has decreased over the years. In 1900 there were approximately 10,000 wild elephants. Today it is estimated that there are up to 3,000 elephants in Sri Lanka.

The leopard is the island's top predator. No lions or tigers steal its kill, as happens to leopards in Africa and India. The Sri Lankan leopard knows no bounds. It ranges from the Horton Plains to the wet-zone forests and sometimes ventures near upcountry estates.

More than 400 species of birds have been sighted in Sri Lanka; 26 are indigenous species. Most are resident, like the spot-billed pelican, but some migrate seasonally. More than 450 fish species, including the black ruby and cherry barb, red-tailed goby, and green pufferfish, populate Sri Lanka's rivers, marshes, and coastal waters.

There are more than 170 reptile species, 101 endemic. Sri Lanka's reptiles include the star tortoise, marsh crocodile, and five species of turtle, all protected. Snakes abound in the forests, the lethal species being the cobra, Russell's and saw-scaled viper, and Indian and Ceylon krait.

Sri Lanka is an amphibian hotspot, with more than 250 species of frogs—about 10 percent of all frog species in the world.

CONSERVATION

Providing refuge to so many species of indigenous wildlife, some of which are facing extinction, Sri Lanka's ecosystems need to be protected. The Department of Wildlife Conservation and the Department of Forestry look after more than 20 national parks and other protected areas, the latter focusing on forest reserves.

The Coast Conservation Department works to reduce coastal damage. Erosion is a particularly serious problem on the southern beaches, which face the Indian Ocean and are hit by waves from the open sea. Coral reefs serve as natural breakwaters, but scuba diving, coral mining, and other human activities pollute and damage the reefs.

Environmental groups have been set up in more than 3,000 schools across the island to nurture an environmentally friendly generation of Sri Lankans. By taking part in projects and writing reports, children learn about managing and protecting the environment and about living in an environmentally responsible way.

POLLUTION AND FLOODING

The main environmental problems Sri Lanka faces include urban air pollution and water pollution, erosion and flooding, and indiscriminate garbage disposal.

Factories are required by law to obtain a license from the CEA before starting operations. The CEA grants a license after checking that proper pollution control systems are in place. Existing plants without such systems are expected to install them within a specified period. There is a growing market for pollution prevention equipment.

Deforestation, the disappearance of forest cover, leads to river bank erosion, increasing the severity of floods that are already a problem because of shifting coastal sand bars and lagoons that affect river exits to the sea. Deforestation and climate change are expected to gradually increase the frequency of drought, especially in the dry zone.

Many parts of Sri Lanka lack the resources and infrastructure for waste management. The large towns depend on municipal garbage collectors, while in Colombo, a private firm sees to the cleanliness of the city. Uncontrolled dumping is a widespread occurrence, creating breeding grounds for pests such as rats and mosquitoes. Dumping of garbage in open areas pollutes ground and surface water, while open burning of waste contributes to air pollution, posing serious health risks.

A public health inspector assigned by the Ministry of Health sees to solid waste management in the municipal and urban councils. At the national level, the MFE and CEA draw up and enact policies concerning solid waste. The National Environmental Act restricts waste emission, while the local authorities are responsible for the proper removal of municipal solid waste and its disposal at suitable dumping areas.

ENERGY

Sri Lanka declared 1999 to 2009 the decade of power development. New power plants and an improved national grid were built to provide every household with access to electricity and increase the efficiency of power distribution. The government attracted private investors to the power sector, controlled by the Ceylon Electricity Board, by providing tax breaks and other incentives.

Today thermal power stations are the largest source of power in Sri Lanka, making up 48 percent of total capacity in 2010. Thermal power stations run on either diesel, gas, or other fuel oils. Most of the oil is imported.

Garbage strewn along a beach. The Sri Lankan government is trying to manage the problem of indiscriminate garbage disposal.

On December 26, 2004, the worst natural disaster in modern times occurred. Following an undersea earthquake off the west coast of Sumatra, a massive tsunami was unleashed around the Indian Ocean that killed an estimated 230,000 people in 14 countries. Waves of up to 100 feet (30 m) high devastated coastal towns and villages in Indonesia, Thailand, India, and Sri Lanka, and were even felt as far away as East Africa. With a magnitude of between 9.1 and 9.3 on the Richter scale, it is the third-largest earthquake recorded on a seismograph (an instrument used to measure movement in the Earth).

In Sri Lanka, the tsunami struck over 600 miles (1,000 km), or two-thirds, of the country's coastline, from Jaffna in the northeast stretching down the east and south coast and as far as Chilaw on the west coast. An estimated 31,000 people were killed and a further half a million people displaced by the natural disaster. More than 88,000 houses were damaged, of which 50,000 were completely destroyed. Fortunately the port of Colombo and the industrial belt in the western province suffered only light damage.

The businesses of many thousands of Sri Lankan fishermen were badly affected, with fishing gear and up to 24,000 boats destroyed by the massive waves. Estimates suggest that the livelihoods of at least 250,000 fishermen were damaged in some way. The tsunami also had an environmental impact, with thousands of rice, mango, and banana plantations swamped by the water. On the island's east coast, the tsunami contaminated wells on which many villagers relied for drinking water.

The international response was generous, and governments and agencies from abroad poured money into the disaster relief effort. USAID and other international aid organizations and charities spent many years rebuilding the infrastructure of the hardest hit areas, as well as rebuilding homes and schools and retraining local people in useful trades. By 2009 the aid effort was complete.

The Norocholai Power Station became Sri Lanka's first coal-powered power station in 2011. By 2014 it is predicted that Norocholai will be the island's largest power-producing plant.

Sri Lanka also relies heavily on hydroelectric power. In 2010 roughly 45 percent of the country's electricity was derived from waterpower. A decade earlier, hydroelectric power had provided 70 percent of the country's power. Although hydroelectric power is a clean form of energy, it has shortcomings. It relies on the volume and strength of rivers, and power cuts have to be imposed whenever the southwest monsoon fails.

Sri Lanka intends to survey its territorial waters for oil deposits. Surveys in the early 1980s indicated possible offshore oil and gas reserves, but economic and political troubles prevented further exploration at the time. Sri Lanka has also sought to develop solar energy, and there is a wind power plant at Hambantota.

INTERNET LINKS

http://earthobservatory.nasa.gov/IOTD/view.php?id=5125

A NASA Earth Observatory photograph shows a part of the Sri Lankan coast just before and just after it was struck by the tsunami.

www.galenfrysinger.com/asian_elephants.htm

This site contains photos and descriptions of elephants in Sri Lanka.

www.environmentlanka.com/

This site provides information, galleries, and discussions on Sri Lankan environment, biodiversity, eco-tourism, and environmental issues.

www.elephant.se/location2.php?location_id=43

This site is dedicated to the elephant orphanage at Pinnewela, and provides a history, data on the elephants there, and photographs.

SRI LANKANS

Sri Lankan girls pose for the camera near the Colombo–Galle express train.

6

S EVERAL ETHNIC GROUPS MAKE UP the Sri Lankan population of more than 21 million. The main groups are the Sinhalese, Tamils, Moors, Burghers, and Veddhas. Other smaller groups make up the minority.

Sri Lankans from each ethnic group can be identified by their names. The most common names among the Sinhalese are Perera and Fernando. Other Sinhalese names such as Senanayake and Bandaranaike are as polysyllabic as Tamil ones such as Selvarajah and Kandasamy.

The Moors typically name their sons Mohammed and Ahmed and their daughters Fathima and Noor. The Burghers have Portuguese- or Dutch-sounding names such as Jansz and Buultjens.

Sri Lankan names usually indicate a person's ethnic group.

The Sinhalese have an Indo-Aryan ancestry, the Tamils a Dravidian ancestry, the Moors an Arab ancestry, and the Burghers a European ancestry. By faith, the Sinhalese, Tamils, Moors, and Burghers are generally Buddhist, Hindu, Muslim, and Christian, respectively.

More than 80 percent of Sri Lankans live in rural areas, since much of the country is given to agriculture. Most Sinhalese live in the southwest; Sri Lankan Tamils in the north and east; and Indian Tamils in the south-central region.

The urban population of Sri Lanka is only 14 percent. Urban clusters include Colombo in the west, Kandy in the south-central hills, Galle in the south, and Jaffna in the north. The number of migrants to cities and industrial zones is rising.

The population growth rate is low, at 0.9 percent. With a falling birthrate and low death rate, the proportion of young dependents (below the age of 15 years) in the population is falling while that of old dependents (above age 64 years) is rising. Aging is thus a growing concern in the 21st century.

ETHNIC UNREST (1983–2009)

Racism has plagued Sri Lanka for the past two decades. In fact ethnic rivalry existed even before independence, under the divide-and-rule policy of the British. More English schools were set up in the north, especially in Jaffna. As a result more Tamils benefited from an English education, which put them in a better position to be admitted to universities and to study science, medicine, and mathematics. When the British left in 1948, Tamils held most of the well-paid positions in professions such as medicine, engineering, and accounting. (In the 1960s the government tried to close the ethnic gap with a quota system for university entrance. This naturally upset the Tamils.)

In 1956 the Bandaranaike government made Sinhala the official language of the country. Then, in 1958, in response to objections from the Tamils, the government enacted the Reasonable Use of Tamil Act. Tamil became the language used by the administration in the north, in addition to Sinhala used

Sri Lanka's Tamil Tiger guerrillas in training in 1994.

nationally. Tamil and Sinhalese students have received instruction in their respective mother tongues in most schools and universities since 1961.

The emergence of the LTTE fueled ethnic unrest. In 1983 the LTTE killed 13 Sinhalese soldiers. Outraged, the Sinhalese community killed hundreds of Tamils and destroyed Tamil homes and shops. The Tamils turned to the LTTE to fight back, and hatred flared between the ethnic groups. Civil war broke out, and the fighting continued for more than two decades.

During the civil war, the government attempted to negotiate a settlement, granting the Tamils several concessions, short of an independent state called Eelam. The LTTE assassinated several Sinhalese leaders and made an attempt on the life of President Kumaratunga.

In spite of the conflict, day-to-day encounters between many Tamils and Sinhalese remained friendly. They studied and worked together. Even on the outskirts of the area held by the LTTE, Sinhalese and Tamils helped one another harvest the rice fields. In a bid to reduce ethnic division, English is given prominence, even as a medium of instruction in schools. News is

A Sinhalese woman.

published and broadcast in Sinhala, Tamil, and English. Yet the LTTE and, in turn, the armed forces and politicians, kept the flames of war burning. Fortunately, after 26 years, the civil war came to an end in 2009.

THE SINHALESE

The Sinhalese are descendants of the ancient Indo-Aryans of northern India. The legend of Vijaya traces the origin of the Sinhalese to the prince whose father was Sinhabahu. The word *sinha* means "lion," and the Sinhalese like to think they have a leonine ancestry.

The Sinhalese inherited the Indian caste system. One's caste determined one's profession as goldsmith, dancer, tom-tom beater, farmer, fisherman, or clothes washer, called *dhoby* (DHOH-bee). Farmers belonged to a high caste, just below the aristocracy. But Buddhism broke caste barriers, and the Sinhalese now generally ignore caste in work, though not in marriage.

Most urban Sinhalese wear Western-style clothing to work. At home and in the streets and shops, the men wear a shirt over a *sarama* (SAH-rah-mah), a piece of cloth wrapped around the lower body from the waist almost to the ankles. The traditional dress for women is the sari. Rural Sinhalese women wear a blouse and a printed wrap-around. Gold jewelry is a must.

THE TAMILS

Sri Lankan Tamils, commonly known as Jaffna Tamils, live mostly in the north and east of the country, although major towns in other areas also have large Tamil populations. Sri Lankan Tamils claim descent from the Chola, Pandya, and Pallava invaders from southern India. They are Hindus and adhere to the caste system more rigidly than do the Sinhalese.

A Tamil family at Siva Subramania Swami Temple.

Sri Lankan Tamils see themselves as superior to Indian Tamils, who are descendants of the workers imported from India by the British to work on tea and coffee plantations during the colonial years. Indian Tamils live mostly on the tea estates in the south-central hills.

At home, Tamil men may wear a *verti* (VER-tee), similar to a *sarama*, with a collarless shirt. Tamil women, like Sinhalese women, wear the *sari*. Married women wear a *thali* (TAH-lee), a pendant symbolizing the marriage vow, and a *pottu* (PAW-too), a red dot on the forehead that is associated with fertility. The part in the hair is also colored red. Most Tamil women wear jasmine flowers in their hair at weddings and other functions.

MOORS AND BURGHERS

Moors, descendants of Arab traders who settled in Sri Lanka as long ago as the eighth century A.D., live in all parts of the island except in Jaffna. Apart from Moors, descendants of migrant Malays from Southeast Asia make up another Muslim group in Sri Lanka.

Burghers divide themselves into groups according to their ancestry—there are Dutch Burghers, British Burghers, and Portuguese Burghers. They

An indigenous Veddha, or *Wanniya-laeto*, who are thought to be the original inhabitants of the country.

live in the urban areas (the Dutch word *burgher* means "town dweller") and follow a Western lifestyle.

When Sinhalese nationalism swept through the land in the 1950s, and Sinhala and then Tamil, rather than English, were adopted as the languages of instruction in schools, many Burgher families emigrated, mainly to Australia.

VEDDHAS

The aboriginal Veddhas live in the forests of the Uva basin east of the south-central hills. They have short curly hair and broad noses, like the aboriginal bushmen of Australia and the pygmies of Africa.

The Veddhas call themselves *Wanniya-laeto*, or "forest dwellers." The word *veddha* (VAYD-hah) in Sinhala means "hunter." Once believers in spirits, many Veddhas have now converted to Buddhism. They are fast losing their identity as hunter-gatherers, as they are resettled in villages and forced to give up hunting. Instead they cultivate land on the jungle fringes, living on game, honey, and the produce of their plots.

In the late 1970s the government began clearing Veddha ancestral lands to make way for the Mahaweli Diversion Project. In 1983 more land was taken from the Veddhas and turned into the Maduru Oya National Park.

Due to international interest in the plight of the Veddhas, the government declared in 1998 that the Veddhas could return to their ancestral land.

However, returning Veddhas have found intruders, such as poachers and loggers who rob the forest of game and timber.

GYPSIES

The gypsies live in groups of a few families under a leader. They are nomadic, living in temporary shelters made out of leaves and loading their clothes, cooking pots, chickens, and other belongings on the backs of donkeys when traveling to a new location.

The gypsies have their own system of government, with a chief justice in Anuradhapura. They meet annually to discuss matters such as travel routes. Each group specializes in a craft or service. For example, the Ahikuntakaya trap snakes and charm them with the movement (not the music) of their pipes. Other groups may carve their niche in tattooing, telling fortunes, making beads, hats, or reed baskets, training monkeys to dance, and so on.

INTERNET LINKS

http://countrystudies.us/sri-lanka/38.htm

This site provides an introduction to the various ethnic groups in Sri Lanka, including the Sinhalese, the Tamils, the Muslims, the Burghers, and the Veddhas.

http://vedda.org/

This site is dedicated to the Veddhas of Sri Lanka, with details of the history of the people with photographs.

www.lankalibrary.com/cul.html

This is the official website of the Virtual Library of Sri Lanka. It includes information about the main ethnic groups as well as the others such as the Yakkas and Nagas, the Muslims and Moors, the Malay, the Ceylon Jews, the Colombo Chetties, and the gypsies. It also includes a section on naming conventions and the caste system.

http://withanage.tripod.com/history.htm

This website contains a short history of the people of Sri Lanka with a focus on the nation's early history, its European connections, and British connections.

LIFESTYLE

A crowded street in Sri Lanka's capital city of Colombo.

7

THE ANCESTRAL HERITAGE OF EACH of Sri Lanka's ethnic groups has given them different customs and practices that have been passed down from one generation to the next.

The different faiths that the Sinhalese, Tamils, Moors, and Burghers profess have also greatly influenced their behavior. In addition the villager and the urbanite adhere to tradition to varying degrees.

Since Sri Lankans have different lifestyles and patterns of behavior, it is nearly impossible when describing any one group of Sri Lankans to say, "This is the lifestyle of the Sri Lankans." However, there are certain values that the different ethnic groups share.

Sri Lankan values include love and respect for family, hospitality, impetuosity, and cleanliness.

Sri Lankan women taking a bath in the river near Nuwara Eliya.

Family is very important to Sri Lankans and family members, including extended family, are usually quite close.

For example, all Sri Lankans take pride in their families. The Sri Lankan family unit is close-knit and often an extended family, in which a young couple normally lives under one roof with their parents, aunts, uncles, grandparents, and sometimes even great-grandparents.

Children are doted on. Babies are hardly ever left to cry; many are indulged as much as possible. Wealthy couples used to employ *ayahs* (AH-yahs), or nannies, to take care of their children.

Today, however, young working mothers often put their careers on hold to look after their young children. They are entitled to 84 days of paid maternity leave for the first two children and 42 days for the third and subsequent. In any case, relatives are often around to lend a hand.

SHARED VALUES

RESPECT Another value Sri Lankans share is respect for the elderly. Families take good care of their old relatives and make efforts to ensure that they feel wanted. There are retirement homes for the elderly, of course, but it is usually people with no relatives who live in these homes. Those with a family are seldom left to live alone. Sri Lankan children are brought up with the idea that it is their duty to care for their parents. Buddhism, a major religion in Sri Lanka, emphasizes this duty.

Showing respect extends to other seniors and people of higher social status as well. Children respect their parents, students respect their teachers, and society respects monks, nuns, and priests. When talking to a monk, one shows respect by folding the hands in prayer and bowing. One does not touch a monk.

Students show respect to their school principal by standing up when the principal walks into the classroom. On the first day of school, a student may greet the teacher with a sheaf of betel leaves and kneel, palms closed. The same salutation is made when greeting one's parents at the New Year or when inviting relatives to one's wedding.

HOSPITALITY Sri Lankans can be hospitable or irritable, depending on the time and place. Waiting in a bus line or weaving through a shopping crowd, for example, people may find it hard to avoid an argument and may react "as if a fly went past the nose," to use the Sinhala saying. (Sri Lanka in the hot season is full of flies.)

No matter how humble, the Sri Lankan home is invariably a place for sharing and caring. Visitors are always invited to stay for a meal, and foreign guests are treated with special graciousness.

CLEANLINESS Cleanliness is godliness to most Sri Lankans. Sri Lankans are avid bathers, probably because the weather is tropical and cool water is plentiful. Streams, rivers, beaches, and swimming pools are always crowded.

BIRTH THROUGH CHILDHOOD

Every pregnancy is regarded as a blessing in Sri Lanka. The island may be overpopulated, the government may encourage family planning, but to any family, a new baby is always welcome. A pregnant woman is likely to be fussed

A Sri Lankan woman with her child.

over by her family, who will try to allay her craving for an exotic or unusual food. Her mother, grandmother, or mother-in-law will supervise her meals. Her colleagues and friends will shower her with pickles, chutney, and fresh fruit.

The baby is usually delivered in a hospital or maternity home. Even villages have their own maternity homes. There was a time when births took place at home, with a midwife in attendance. Infant mortality was high then. It is not the custom in Sri Lanka to throw a baby shower, but visitors bring gifts for the baby soon after birth.

FIRST RICE AND FIRST LESSON Tamil and Sinhalese parents make a ritual of a baby's first meal of boiled rice. This usually happens when the baby is around eight months old. Hindus feed the baby the first mouthful of milk rice in the *kovil* (KOH-vil), or Hindu temple.

The Sinhalese lay a mat on the floor with dishes of *kiributh* (ki-ri-booth)—milk rice, bananas, traditional sweets, a book, and a piece of jewelry. The baby is allowed to crawl on the mat and choose one item. If the baby reaches for the book, everyone says they are in the presence of a future scholar or intellectual. If the piece of jewelry is picked, the baby shows promise of wealth and prosperity. If an item of food is grabbed, everyone fears the baby will become a bum!

At about the age of two years, it is customary for the child to have his or her first lesson. The lesson is given at a predetermined auspicious hour by a learned relative, the temple monk, or the principal of the local school.

GROWING UP

Traditionally a family celebration marked each milestone in the life of the individual. Sharing personal experiences with family members, especially parents, helped to strengthen bonds. But many families now ignore the rituals that form part of such celebrations.

A Sinhalese or Tamil girl celebrates her coming-of-age and eligibility for marriage with her family. In a traditional Tamil home, the young girl stays in seclusion for about 16 days. In a traditional Sinhalese home, too, she avoids normal activity, and it is considered bad luck for her to look upon a male, even a brother. Then at the appointed time, the girl is bathed by a *dhoby*, who pours water over her from a clay pot and then dashes the pot to the ground. The girl receives gifts, often cash or jewelry.

There is no special ceremony for a boy attaining puberty, unless he is Muslim, in which case he is circumcised in his early teens.

MARRIAGE

Married life is the preference for most Sri Lankan women; staying single is not seen as a desirable option. Although teen marriages used to be common, Sri Lankans now marry at a later age for economic reasons.

A bridegroom and bride dressed in traditional Kandyan attire.

Arranged marriages are still practiced in Sri Lanka. Originally a *magul kapuwa* (MAH-gool KAH-poo-wah), a marriage broker, would visit the parents of an eligible young man or woman and help the parents "fix up" their son or daughter. These days, with the *magul kapuwa* almost extinct, Sri Lankans turn to relatives and friends for assistance in matchmaking and advertising in the newspapers for potential wives and husbands.

Marriage mediators propose candidates and look into their

A Hindu woman undergoing marriage rites.

morals and credentials. Dowries are settled discreetly. Though the groom would like his bride to bring a dowry, he prefers not to ask for it. It is up to the bride's parents to endow her with cash, jewelry, and a house. A Tamil custom even allows the man to use part of his wife's dowry to settle his own sister in marriage.

Wedding celebrations can be a big affair. A village wedding may last for days, while the urban rich patronize big hotels. Most couples prefer to invite only their closest relatives and friends to their home. The tradition is for the couple to go to the groom's home after the celebration in the bride's home, and the bride's immediate family visits her the next day. There is also a post-honeymoon party at the groom's home.

Tamils usually marry in the temple, but if the wedding is in a hotel, a priest performs the ceremony before the guests. Muslims celebrate the wedding at the bride's home or at a hotel. Burghers marry in church and hold a reception after the ceremony. Many Christian Sinhalese follow the same practice.

HOROSCOPES: ANCIENT CONSULTANT

A horoscope is cast by an astrologer, who takes the time of birth as the basis for prediction. The time of birth determines the zodiac sign, as well as whether the person is deva *(DAY-veh),* manussa *(mah-NOOS-seh), or* raksha *(RUK-shah), meaning "godly," "human," or "devilish," respectively.*

Horoscopes are written on a chart or an ola *(OH-lah) scroll made of a cured piece of talipot palm leaf. Good and bad periods in a person's life are recorded.*

When a marriage is proposed, the horoscopes of the couple are compared as the very first step. If more than half of 20 "conditions" are favorable, the union can go through with no disastrous results.

Horoscopes are read by an astrologer at various stages and events in a person's life: at birth, at puberty, for an examination or a new job, when choosing a spouse, for a new house, or for any other important decision that has to be made. Horoscopes are a guide from the heavens.

THE WEDDING CEREMONY

There is an auspicious time, chosen by an astrologer, for every step of a Sinhalese Buddhist wedding ceremony. The couple gets married in a *poruwa* (POH-roo-wah), a decorated structure like a house. The bride's maternal uncle guides the rituals. The little fingers of the groom's left and the bride's right hand are tied together with gold thread, and water from a silver urn is poured over the knot to symbolize sharing. The bride is dressed in rich silks and lots of jewelry. A Kandyan bride wears the traditional seven *padakkam* (PAH-dah-kum), or pendants, starting with a choker and ending with a chain reaching the knees. The items of jewelry she wears are mostly heirlooms; her family may go into debt just to dress her on her wedding day.

DEATH AND FUNERALS

Buddhists and Hindus cremate their dead; Christians and Muslims bury theirs. However, many Christians are now opting for cremation.

Headstones in a cemetery by Pamunugama beach.

When wood was cheap, a pyre of special timber was built. Now gas crematoriums are used in big cities. Funerals in Sri Lanka tend to be expensive. Except for Muslims, who hold the funeral within 24 hours of a person's death, most Sri Lankans have their dead embalmed and keep the body in the house or funeral parlor for relatives and friends to pay their last respects. In villages the entire community turns out to pay their respects to the deceased and to comfort the bereaved.

For economic reasons, however, funerals are becoming simpler, with the exception of state funerals for political figures and religious persons of high rank. Many non-Muslims now hold a funeral within a day of a person's death. Some people choose to have their bodies donated after death to a medical faculty for research, thus saving their families the expense of even a coffin.

Buddhists observe last rites for the dead called the *pansakula* (PUN-seh-cool-leh). Monks are invited to the cemetery or to the home where the body lies. They chant a verse in Pali that says all things are transient, all things decay and pass away. A sermon is preached to comfort the mourners, who give 60 feet (18 m) of white cloth to the temple.

The nearest relatives pour water from a jug into a bowl so that it spills over, signifying the transference of merit to the dead. The greater the merit, the better the chance of rebirth in a good place as a human being. As part of the custom, two nephews of the dead person circle the pyre or crematorium three times before the cremation. The day after the cremation, the ashes of the body are collected in a clay urn and later buried.

Dané (DAH-neh), meaning "alms," is given to the temple on the seventh day after death. Three months later and on every anniversary of the death, monks are invited to the home of the bereaved for almsgiving. This is believed to confer merit on the dead person and also on the living, who by this act of giving lessen their craving for material things.

HOROSCOPES AND AYURVEDIC MEDICINE

A horoscope becomes important when someone is ill and needs to consult an Ayurvedic doctor.

Folk medicine, or the use of herbal and traditional cures, is a thriving practice in Sri Lanka. So important is this 2,500-year-old practice that there are five times as many doctors practicing Ayurvedic medicine in Sri Lanka as Western medicine. There is even a government ministry responsible for Ayurvedic medicine.

An Ayurvedic cure treats the whole patient, not just the ailment. Even the person's horoscope and temperament are relevant. Herbs, roots, and spices are taken as medicine. A tea of ginger and coriander, for example, may be prescribed for the common cold.

It is commonly believed by Sri Lankans that when Western drugs fail, it is time to resort to Ayurvedic cures. Many Sri Lankans believe that both Western and Ayurvedic medicines can be used simultaneously. This is why pharmacies stock both Western drugs and Ayurvedic herbs. The World Health Organization acknowledges that both branches of medicine can learn much from each other.

A Christian funeral consists of a service held in church, followed by the burial at the cemetery. The coffin is lowered into a hole in the ground, and those present throw handfuls of soil on the coffin, signifying "ashes to ashes, dust to dust."

Muslims carry their dead to the cemetery on a covered wicker stretcher and bury their dead without a coffin.

The few Zoroastrians in Sri Lanka leave their unburied dead to be consumed by vultures in a section of the cemetery set apart for this.

EDUCATION AND EMPLOYMENT

Before colonization, Buddhist monks were the only teachers on the island. During the colonial period, schools run by Portuguese Roman Catholic and

Dutch and British Protestant missions were favored by those aspiring to jobs in the government service.

In the 1960s Sinhala was made the national language. This, it is thought, was the major cause of the ethnic strife instigated by the Tamil minority. English is now being given recognition and emphasis.

Education is free. The literacy rate is 92 percent for men and 90 percent for women, the highest by far in South Asia. More girls attend schools and universities than do boys. Women may enter any profession, even the air force, and they have risen to the top of their professions in the public sector. The private sector, however, still seems to prefer male chief executive officers. In the lower pay scales of the labor market, women have the more menial jobs, like plucking tea leaves on estates and running machines in garment factories.

Sri Lankans can legally enter the labor market once they reach the age of 18 years. However, there are children illegally employed in households and on plantations, and the government is seeking to improve policy measures and raise public awareness on this issue.

The retirement age is 55 years, but senior workers may, at the employer's discretion, choose to continue in their positions beyond age 55.

Most Sri Lankans are employed in agriculture, and their jobs revolve around the seasons. Many plantation workers live "on site," in barrack-like quarters, often one family to a room.

The work pattern is more regular in urban areas, especially in the industrial and service sectors. Much of the labor force works in the tourism industry in hotels, for transportation companies and arts and crafts shops, and at tourist attractions.

Office workers work eight to ten hours a day, with a one-hour break. Saturday is a half day five hours. The overtime wage rate is one-and-a-half times the normal rate, and everyone gets 14 days of paid vacation.

Women are employed in all sectors, but they dominate the lower-paying jobs. Tea-picking, one of the lowest-paid jobs, is mostly done by women. About 80 percent of the factory workers in the trade zones are young single women who live in nearby boarding houses.

Unemployment is a problem, particularly in the shanty towns around the larger cities such as Colombo. Slum occupants try to find work wherever they can, such as helping at shops as packers and loaders. Many of the unemployed have migrated to countries like the United States and Southeast Asia in search of work. In rural areas, the Sarvodaya movement addresses unemployment by awakening in villagers a sense of their own power and ability. A Sarvodaya work camp mobilizes the community to improve its own living conditions.

HEALTH SERVICES

Sri Lanka has a free health service, and a network of hospitals and dispensaries spread over the island. There are also private hospitals and clinics for those who can afford the charges.

INTERNET LINKS

http://findarticles.com/p/articles/mi_m2267/is_3_69/ai_94227137/

This site contains an article about the changing role of women in Sri Lankan society.

www.infolanka.com/photo/fest.html

This website on village life in Sri Lanka covers topics such as rural scenic beauty, festivals, historical sites, wildlife, and art.

www.kwintessential.co.uk/resources/global-etiquette/srilanka.html

This website provides a helpful introduction to etiquette and customs in Sri Lanka, including tips on meeting and greeting, gift giving, dining etiquette, as well as business etiquette and protocol.

www.sarvodaya.org/

This is the official website of the Sarvodaya Shramadana Movement— the largest people's organization in Sri Lanka.

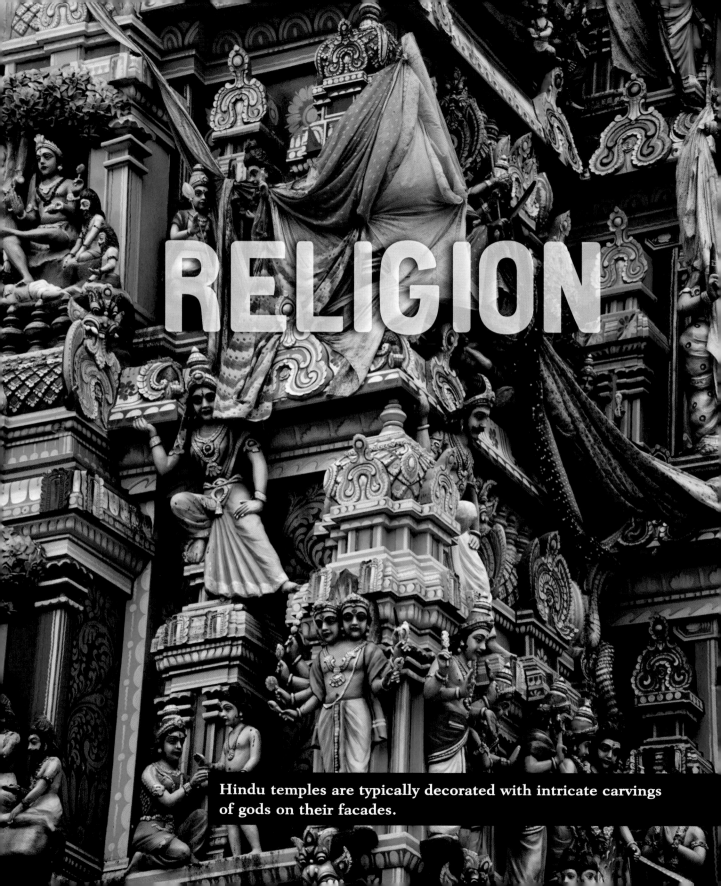

RELIGION

Hindu temples are typically decorated with intricate carvings of gods on their facades.

8

ONE RESULT OF THE COUNTRY'S mixed religious heritage is that the faiths—Buddhism, Hinduism, Islam, and Christianity—have borrowed rituals and symbols from one another.

For example, the Buddha is believed to be one of the 10 reincarnations of Vishnu, a Hindu deity. The *thali*, the symbolic marriage necklace of Tamil Hindus, is also used by Sri Lankan Muslims. As for Sinhalese and Tamils who profess to be Christian, their ancestors having been converted by the Portuguese, Dutch, or British, the Sinhalese are influenced by Buddhist ethics, while Tamil Christians are influenced by their Hindu heritage.

BUDDHISM

The Sinhala Dynasty, as legend has it, was founded by Prince Vijaya on the day the Buddha died in India. To Sri Lankans, this means they

Carvings of a standing and reclining Buddha carved into a rock face at Gal Vihara.

A monk lighting incense at Sri Maha Bodhi in Anuradhapura.

have an inherited role as protector of Buddhism. But it was really much later, about 250 B.C., that Buddhism came to Sri Lanka through Mahinda, the son of Emperor Asoka. A few significant events followed, which entrenched the religion in Sri Lanka.

Asoka's daughter, Sanghamitta, brought a sapling from the bo tree under which Prince Siddhartha (who later became the Buddha) was sitting when he attained enlightenment. The princess founded the Bhikkuni Order, an order of nuns, in Sri Lanka.

In the fourth century A.D., Princess Hemamala of India escaped to Sri Lanka with the Buddha's sacred left eyetooth concealed in her hair. Subsequently kingship went to whoever possessed the tooth relic. It is now protected and revered in the Dalada Maligawa, or Temple of the Tooth, in Kandy. A replica is paraded in Kandy once a year at the Esala Perahera. Another historic event was the writing of the sacred Buddhist scriptures on ola leaves at the Aluvihare Temple cave in Matale, north of Kandy.

At various periods in Sri Lanka's history, while South Indian invaders pillaged stupas and temples and enthusiastic colonizers converted the local population, Buddhism was hidden away in isolated temples, protected and preserved by devout monks. Yet, from the third century B.C. until today, Theravada Buddhism in its purest form, adhering strictly to the original Pali preachings of the Buddha, continues to be practiced on the island.

BUDDHIST WAYS

Buddhism is a way of life. Upon attaining enlightenment on the full moon night of the month of May, the Buddha realized four noble truths: the existence of suffering, its cause, its eradication, and the Eightfold Path to *Nibbana* (nib-HAH-nah).

To Buddhists, the Buddha is a teacher and guide, a human being who found a way to self-deliverance. Buddhist statues, temples, shrines, and the sacred bo tree are venerated with offerings of flowers, the burning of incense

HOW BUDDHISM CAME TO SRI LANKA

Around 250 B.C., while in hot pursuit of a deer in the Mihintale hills, close to his capital, King Devanampiya Tissa heard his name called. He stopped dead in his tracks. Who dared address him so familiarly? He saw a yellow-robed monk who introduced himself as Mahinda, son of Emperor Asoka. He had come from India to teach Buddhism to the people.

Mahinda tested the king with a riddle about mango trees, one not easily understood.

"King, what is this tree called?"

"It is an amba *(AHM-ba) tree." (Amba means "mango.")*

"Besides this amba *tree, is there any other* amba *tree?"*

"There are many other amba *trees."*

"Besides this amba *tree and those other* amba *trees, are there any other trees on Earth?"*

"There are many trees, but they are not amba *trees."*

"Besides the other amba *trees and the trees that are not* amba, *is there any other?"*

"Gracious Lord, this amba!"

Thus the king showed himself capable of understanding the Dhamma (DHAHM-mah), the truth revealed by the Buddha. Mahinda preached a sermon, and the king and his people became Buddhists. He accepted a royal invitation to live on the island, but rejected a magnificent temple in favor of his cave in Mihintale. After climbing 100 steps, one can still see his rock bed, his bathing pool, and the rock-hewn vessel used for his breakfast gruel.

symbolizing purity, and the lighting of oil lamps, symbols of wisdom and enlightenment. They are reminders of the Buddha's teaching that all things are impermanent.

The four Buddhist holy days, or *poya* (POH-yeh) days, correspond with the phases of the moon. On a full moon *poya* day, besides listening to sermons preached by the monks at the temple, Buddhists observe eight precepts

FIVE AND EIGHT PRECEPTS

Buddhists observe these five precepts daily:

• *not to destroy life*

• *not to take what is not given—in other words, not to steal*

• *not to behave immorally*

• *not to tell an untruth or slander*

• *not to take intoxicating drinks and drugs*

In addition, on special days, Buddhists do not:

• *eat at odd times and particularly not after midday*

• *use perfume and cosmetics, listen to music, or dance*

• *use luxurious chairs and beds*

Bhikku	*(BIK-hoo) means "monk."*
Dané	*(DAH-nay) means "almsgiving."*
Nibbana	*(nib-HAH-nah) means "Nirvana," or the end of the samsaric cycle, when no further births take place. This happens when a person attains enlightenment, as the Buddha did.*
Nikaya	*(nik-HAH-yah) means "Buddhist sect of monks." The caste system exists among monks in the form of different sects. Their beliefs are the same, but their rituals and the way they wear their robes differ a little. Monks of the Siyam Nikaya, established in the mid-18th century, carry umbrellas and wear their robes only over one shoulder. Monks of the Amarapura Nikaya (since 1803) carry umbrellas and cover both shoulders. Monks of the Ramanya Nikaya (since 1835) carry a palm leaf shade and cover both shoulders. As the years of origin suggest, the latter two sects have broken away from the first through disagreement with its rules.*
Pin	*(PIN) means "merit." Merit making is like earning credits. The more merit a Buddhist makes, the greater the likelihood of rebirth into a better life after death. The Buddhist layperson makes merit by giving alms, meditating, and observing all the precepts.*
Sangha	*(SUNG-hah) means "the monastic order."*

—three more than usual on other days. They call for abstinence and simple living. Some Buddhists observe 10 precepts, the extra two being not to deal with money and not to wear ornaments.

HINDUISM

Hindus worship one or many gods according to personal choice or particular needs. Brahmin priests act as spiritual guides to Hindu devotees, who make ritual prayers and offerings of food, flowers, and lighted brass lamps daily and on special occasions.

Hindu deities carried by devotees at a procession at the Munneswaram Temple.

The Vedas, a collection of more than a thousand hymns, are the Hindus' source of religious knowledge. Hindus believe in the caste system, which is strongly linked to reincarnation. They are content with their station in life, believing it to be the result of karma, the reward or punishment for good or bad deeds carried out in their previous lives. They try to do good deeds in this life so that their next life will be that of a high-caste person.

Sri Lankan Hindus worship the full pantheon of Hindu gods, including Brahma the creator; Shiva the destroyer of evil and ignorance; Parvati, wife of Shiva; their two sons, Skanda (or Murugan), the Kataragama god, and Ganesh; Pattini, goddess of health and chastity; and Vishnu, preserver of life. Aiyanar, who guards the forests, crops, tanks, and trees, is a most important god for Tamil farmers in the dry zone.

Most Sri Lankan Hindus are Shaivites, Shiva worshipers who believe in the impermanence of things. There is also a good number of Vaishnavites, Hindus who believe in the supremacy of Vishnu on the island.

Jaffna is the stronghold of Hinduism in Sri Lanka. Hindus worship at temples called *devale* (DAY-veh-leh) and shrines called *kovil* (KHOH-vil).

Hindu temples are designed like the human body, with a head, body, and feet. The temple's main statue is situated in the head, while offerings are made in the body, or stomach, of the temple. The *gopuram* (goh-POO-rehm), a multi-tiered gateway with carved images, is at the feet, where worshipers enter the temple.

ISLAM

Muslims are the most conservative religious group in Sri Lanka. They follow their customs strictly. Like Muslims everywhere, they fast during the month of Ramadan and aim to make a pilgrimage to Mecca at least once in their lives.

Muslims make no material offerings and have no images in their mosques. The words of the Koran guide their spiritual and moral lives, and the hypnotic voice of the *muezzin* (moo-EZ-zin) calling the faithful to prayer five times a day keeps them constantly conscious of their faith.

Every city in Sri Lanka has its own Muslim section, so that Sri Lankan Muslims are never too far from a mosque; its location is marked from afar by a very visible minaret.

A group of Muslim children.

CHRISTIANITY

Christianity came to Sri Lanka with the European colonists, whose active conversion efforts established several denominations on the island, including Anglican, Methodist, Baptist, and Presbyterian.

Roman Catholicism is represented in the coastal areas. The vast majority of Burghers are Christian, and there are Sinhalese and Tamils who consider themselves Christians as well.

THE FOREST SHRINES OF KATARAGAMA

Buddhism does not encourage faith in gods and supplication to them. Yet many Buddhists in Sri Lanka go to Kataragama in the southeast of the island to invoke blessings on themselves. Hindus go there every year to make peace with the Hindu god of war, Skanda or Murugan, for this major god of Kataragama is believed to be fierce and vengeful.

Kataragama is a special place for many historical reasons. First, it is where King Devanampiya Tissa planted the sapling of the bo tree brought to Sri Lanka by Emperor Asoka's daughter. Next King Aggabodhi, chief of Ruhuna, built a Buddhist temple and monastery at Kataragama in A.D. 661. Kataragama has also been the capital of several kings: Lokeswara, Kesadatu, and Vijaya Bahu I.

Several temples exist at Kataragama, including those dedicated to Valli Amma, Thevani Amma, Ganesh, and various other Hindu deities. Muslims from the surrounding villages flock to Kataragama to drink from a spring believed to be the fountain of life. Its water is said to make those who drink it immortal. The waters of the Menik Ganga, a river that runs through the forest at Kataragama, are also believed to be sacred.

Sri Lankans have woven many legends around Kataragama. One tells of the Hindu war god, Skanda or Murugan, arriving in Sri Lanka and looking for a place to stay. He went first to the Tamils, who turned him away. He then went to the Sinhalese, who built for him a shelter of leaves.

To punish the Tamils, Skanda decreed that they should come to Kataragama every year and torture themselves in fulfilling their vows. Thus it has been since that time, 2,000 years ago. Every year, Hindus undergo rituals of self-mortification, such as walking on hot coals or carrying on the shoulders a *kavadi* (KAH-veh-di), a wooden or metal arch decorated with peacock feathers.

Another legend tells of a prince who fell in love with Valli Amma, the daughter of a Veddha chief. Valli Amma rejected the prince, so his brother, knowing that Valli Amma feared elephants, planned to turn himself into one to frighten her so that the prince could come to her rescue and win her heart.

Disguised as a hermit and carrying a pot of magic water that he was to pour over his brother once the plan was carried out, the prince went to meet Valli Amma at Kataragama. But seeing that she was choking on her meal, he rushed to give her a sip of the magic water and dropped the pot. Then his brother appeared as an elephant, and the terrified Valli Amma agreed to go with the prince. Unfortunately the magic water had been spilled, and the prince's brother could never regain his human form.

INTERNET LINKS

http://countrystudies.us/sri-lanka/43.htm

This site provides an overview of the religion of Hinduism as practiced in Sri Lanka.

www.accesstoinsight.org/lib/authors/perera/wheel100.html

This website deals with the history of Buddhism in Sri Lanka from the time of its introduction in 250 B.C. up to contemporary times.

www.srilankanchristians.com/

This is the official website of Sri Lankan Christians—an organization that works to ensure freedom of religion, worship, and practice for all Christians in Sri Lanka.

LANGUAGE

A sign at a cashew nut stall in both English and Sinhalese.

9

L ANGUAGE IS A CONTROVERSIAL issue in Sri Lanka. It has, from time to time, been manipulated for political ends. Even today language is a point of division between the Sinhalese and the Tamils.

During the British colonial period, English was the official language. This split Sri Lankans into the English-educated and those who spoke indigenous languages. In 1956 Sinhala became the official language. After much Tamil agitation, the 1978 constitution stated that Tamil would be a national language, though Sinhala would remain the official language.

English is the language of government and is spoken fluently by about 10 percent of the population.

A typist offers a typing service on a street in Colombo.

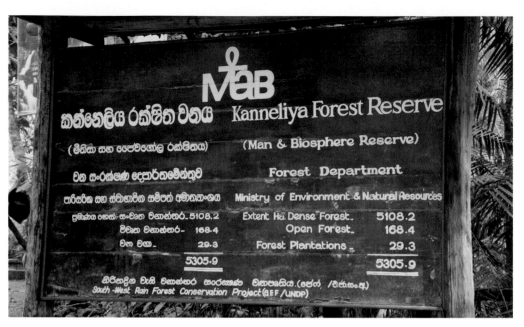

A bilingual sign (Sinhalese and English) at the Kanneliya Forest Reserve.

Sinhala is the language of administration throughout Sri Lanka, but Tamil serves the same function in the northern and eastern parts of the country, where large Tamil populations reside. Schools have introduced a "link language," English, as a second language for all students, while Sinhala and Tamil are third languages for Tamil and Sinhalese children, respectively. Most signboards and notices in Sri Lanka are in three languages: Sinhala, Tamil, and English.

SINHALA

Sinhala is spoken by 74 percent of the Sri Lankan population. Everyone in the country, except perhaps the Western-educated urbanites, can communicate in Sinhala.

Old Sinhala had its origin in Prakrit, an ancient Indian language. In the second century B.C., the influence of Sanskrit changed the indigenous language. The written form was in Brahmi, also known as Asokan script. This writing can still be seen on preserved stone inscriptions. With the arrival of Buddhism in the third century B.C., Prakrit came under the influence of Pali.

In spoken Sinhala, specific forms of address indicate the relationship between the person speaking and the person being addressed. For example, the word you *has several nuances.*

Mé or Oi (may or oh-ee) is used to attract a person's attention.

Numbe (NOOM-beh) is formal and used among equals.

Oya (OH-yeh) is informal and used among friends.

Thamunnaansé (tha-MOON-NAHN-say) is used to address a superior, monk, VIP, or other respected person. Politicians directly address their audiences with this word.

Thamusé (tha-MOO-say) is a less polite "you" that carries nuances of derision and annoyance.

Tho (THOH) is very derogatory. It is used when addressing a person of very low caste or when in the vilest of moods.

Umba (OOM-beh) is used to address menials and servants. Parents also address their children with this word, as it connotes closeness. Domestic helpers resent the word, but those in ancestral homes would be amazed if they were addressed otherwise.

The Sinhala that is used today is more than 20 centuries old. It has 56 curved and artistically complicated letters. The spoken and written forms of the language are somewhat different, though there have been attempts to make written Sinhala less formal. There are also Sinhala dialects. Sinhala spoken by Sri Lankans in Kandy in the hill country is different from that spoken on the island's coast, both in intonation and in the words used.

ENGLISH

Sri Lankans have colored their spoken English with direct translations of Sinhala expressions, such as "I'll go and come" and "what for the telling," that English speakers elsewhere would have difficulty understanding. Journalists and writers, however, stay closer to the standard English used in the United Kingdom.

BODY LANGUAGE

Sri Lankans are restrained in their hand gestures. This is very evident in movies and television dramas. Even singers stand almost immobile. To compensate, facial expressions exaggerate even subtle feelings. But when it comes to love, gestures and movement play a big role in conveying the message: Glances are exchanged, bodies draw near. In formula movies, the hero and heroine in love break into a spirited romp in the bushes, across ponds, and down inclines! Here are the other nonverbal signals Sri Lankans use:

GREETING *Salutation is dignified. The traditional way is to* namaste *(neh-MEHS-tay): bring the palms together at chest level and bend slightly from the waist. People greet a parent, teacher, or religious person by going down on the knees and bending forward right down to the floor with palms together in the* namaste *position.*

HEAD WOGGLE *To say "yes," the head moves from side to side with a down-up, not a sharp left-right, movement. Indians have a similar head gesture signifying agreement.*

HAND HOLDING *Sri Lankans hold hands when they walk with friends. The sight of two men or women walking thus entwined in Sri Lanka does not surprise observers or suggest sexual intimacy.*

SITTING *It is rude to sit on a higher seat than an elder or better, or with legs stretched out pointing to a shrine or monk. Legs are neatly tucked away.*

WALKING *It used to be the norm for men to walk, swinging their arms freely, while their wives followed respectfully, carrying baby and baggage. Today, in villages and towns, many women still walk behind, but are no longer beasts of burden. Servants never walk abreast of their employers.*

TAMIL

About 18 percent of the population speaks Tamil. Although Sinhala is spoken only in Sri Lanka, Tamil is used by people in other countries as well. It is spoken in the South Indian state of Tamil Nadu, Sri Lanka's closest neighbor in India, as well as in several other Asian countries, such as Malaysia and Singapore, where there are populations of South Indian origin.

ARABIC

For Muslims, whether they are Moor or Malay, Arabic is the language of religious instruction and prayer. The Moors generally speak Tamil and usually opt to be educated in Tamil. The Malays retain their mother tongue, Malay. Many Malay students choose Sinhala as their medium of instruction, because Malay is not used in school.

INTERNET LINKS

www.freewebs.com/slageconr/9thicslsflpprs/fullp126.pdf

This article entitled "Sri Lankan English: Exploding the Fallacy" explores the Sri Lankan variety of the English language.

www.lanka.info/dictionary/EnglishToSinhala.jsp

This site contains a useful online dictionary of about 28,335 words in English translated to Sinhala and Tamil. It also includes a pronunciation guide.

www.speaksinhala.com/

This unique website helps people learn spoken Sinhala. The lessons consist of grammar structures, functional language, and vocabulary. It also includes sound files to help with pronunciation.

ARTS

A dancer performs a traditional dance.

10

THE PAINTINGS AND CRAFTS OF
Sri Lanka are a kaleidoscope of color and intricacy, of styles and forms. They employ a mixture of tradition and innovation. Some of them have a religious and often ritualistic foundation, used with dance and song to celebrate sacred events.

The arts of Sri Lanka, including painting, music, dance, and drama, are largely influenced by nature and Buddhism.

The professionals of Sri Lanka's traditional arts scene were caste-based. This means that dancers were of one caste, jewelers of another, pottery makers of a third, and so on. For instance, drummers came from the

A classical fresco of a jewel merchant. Sri Lanka has a rich history of the arts that can be seen through numerous ancient frescoes that have been discovered.

berawaya (bear-ah-WAH-yah) caste, and no other caste took to drumming as a means of livelihood or even as a pastime. The castes to which artists belonged were below the farmers and the aristocracy.

This has changed now with the existence of colleges and youth centers that emphasize the arts. Traditional arts, which would have faded away if they had been left to be passed on from generation to generation, are thus enjoying a revival with young Sri Lankans.

The freedom for anyone to practice the arts has eliminated a monopoly on the arts or on any one art form by caste or dynasty. Art is also being promoted by the government and by private enterprise through the sponsorship of exhibitions abroad.

DANCE

There are two Sinhalese dance styles: low country and hill country. Low-country dance combines elements of mime, dramatic dialogue, and impersonation, and the dancers often wear strange and scary masks.

A group of traditional dancers hold their poses after a performance.

A couple from the Kaffir community dancing in Colombo.

Performed in the coastal belt south of Colombo, low-country dancing usually features exorcism. For example, the devil dance, which may last 12 hours, weaves together humor and frightening images to heal the sick. Exorcism is a carefully crafted ritual that originated in Sri Lanka's pre-Buddhist era. It incorporates ancient Ayurvedic ideas about the causes of disease. The frightening demon mask worn by the devil dancer is believed to be both the cause of and the cure for the illness. In the *bali* (BAH-li) dance, the dancer talks to the evil spirit that has possessed the sick person to draw out the spirit and chase it away.

Both low-country and hill-country styles use vigorous movements and traditional costumes. Hill-country dances have classical origins and have been passed down in traditional Kandyan dancing families from father to son for many generations. The Kandyan dancer wears yards of frilly white red-trimmed cloth, a beaded breastplate, and an intricate silver headdress. Bells around his ankles jingle, as the dancer pirouettes, skips, whirls, and stamps his feet to the rhythm of the drums. Kandyan dance involves a lot of acrobatic cartwheels and leaps. The *vannama* (veh-NAH-meh) imitates the movements of animals. Watching the *gajaba* (geh-JAH-beh) *vannama*, for instance, one can clearly see the movements of a majestic elephant.

The Tamils retain Indian classical dances such as *bharatanatyam*. The Burghers prefer Western dances such as ballroom styles and ballet. The *kaffringa* and *baila* dance styles introduced by the Portuguese are popular at parties, and even five-star hotels have *baila* sessions.

THE BEAT OF THE DRUM

The usual Sri Lankan musical ensemble includes drums with tiny cymbals and a conch shell or horn pipe called *horaneva* (HOR-ah-NAY-vah). Cylindrical or conical drums, *bera* (BAY-rah), have wooden frames with animal skins stretched over the opening. They are tapped with the fingers and palm or else beaten with a cane stick. Some common drums are the *geta* (get-teh) *bera*, *devale* (DAY-vah-leh) *bera*, and *yak* (yuk) *bera* used in devil-dancing.

Urban Sri Lankans enjoy Western music. Orchestras play classical music. Jazz has not caught on much. Several musicians who are popular in Sri Lanka and abroad sing Sinhalese and Tamil songs.

Kandyan drummers preparing for a performance. Drums are an integral part of Sri Lankan music.

THEATER

Four varieties of Sri Lankan folk drama have evolved. The *sokari* (sew-KAH-ri) is an adaptation of rituals once performed for an abundant harvest. In the almost extinct *nadagam* (NAH-deh-gum) and *kavi* (KAH-vi) *nadagam* from Ambalangoda, a narrator relates the story as masked dancers portray the characters. The fourth variety, *kolam* (KOH-lum), is an all-night event.

Contemporary theater is alive in all three languages, but predominantly in Sinhala. Local English-language productions range from original drama to Shakespearean plays to spectacular musicals like *Les Misérables*.

Pots serve as both art and function in Sri Lanka with households using pots to store water.

Sri Lankans watch films in English, Tamil, and Hindi. Since Lester James Peiris's *Rekawa* in the 1950s, quality Sinhala films have also been screened in Sri Lankan movie theaters. In patronage of the arts, the government renovated and refurbished an old theater, the Tower Hall, and a cinema hall, the Elphinstone, both in Colombo.

CRAFTS

METALWORK AND POTTERY The island has a long tradition of metal-work using gold, silver, copper, tin, and alloys such as bronze. A traditional Tamil wedding custom involves the groom tying a gold wedding necklace, called a *thali*, around the bride's neck. The Kandyan bride is required to wear seven items of jewelry around her neck.

Pottery is a living craft, practiced in homes and temples. Every household has a pitcher or big-bellied clay pot to store water. Temples have clay oil lamps, and clay vessels were traditionally used for cooking.

Sri Lanka's exciting contemporary art scene is little known outside the island. Artists including Muhanned Cader, Druvinka, and Sanjeewa Kumara are well-established names, but other emerging artists such as Vajira Gunewardena and Pala Pothupitiye are building a reputation as well. In 2011 these artists participated in a major exhibition featuring more than 25 works, held in London, the first such event since the end of the civil war in 2009.

MASK MAKING This folk art originated in Ambalangoda, south of Colombo. Devil-dance masks are carved from wood and painted in shocking colors. They come in various sizes, depending on their use: The souvenirs are small, while those for ceremonies fit the head and those for ornaments are oversized. Used in dance, the ritual masks have a hypnotic effect. Collectors see them as artistic masterpieces. Each mask has the face of a particular demon that represents a specific mental or physical illness commonly experienced by the villagers. The identities of the 18 or so core demons differ from area to area, or even across communities in one area.

WOOD AND IVORY CARVING The ancient craft of woodcarving is still actively practiced, mostly by artisans in the Kandy area. Their delicate filigree panels decorate the tops of doors, windows, and tables. Ivory elephants with filigree-worked, gem-encrusted gold or silver coverings, depicting *perahera* (PAIR-ah-HAIR-ah), or festival, elephants testify to the talent and dedication of professional artisans.

STONE SCULPTING This craft was practiced while the ancient royal capitals were at Anuradhapura and Polonnaruwa and the kings were patrons of the arts. There are gigantic, well-proportioned rock statues in both places. It is believed that the magnificent Aukana Buddha, 36 feet (11 m) tall, was built by King Dhatusena in the fifth century A.D. More impressive, though smaller, the Samadhi Pilame, or Meditative Statue, in Anuradhapura greatly inspired the first Indian prime minister, Jawarharlal Nehru. Isurumuniya, also in Anuradhapura, is a picturesque temple with a quiet pool, with two exquisite carvings, one of a rider on a horse, the other of two lovers.

MATS AND BASKETS Mats adorn every rural home and some urban houses, particularly Buddhist ones. Kalutara, a town south of Colombo, displays mats and handicrafts in wayside shops. In the Dumbara valley, close to Kandy, is a village where hempen weaving is an exquisite art.

The island is rich in material for baskets of rattan, bamboo, rush, and palm leaves. Jaffna baskets, justly famous, are made from palmyra leaves and are reputed to be able to hold water. Many kitchens have containers, strainers, food covers, and carpets made of natural products, including coconut coir.

INTERNET LINKS

www.bookrags.com/research/literaturesri-lanka-sinhalese-ema-03/

This short history of literature, written in the Sinhala language, covers the periods from classical Sinhala to colonial domination to independent Sri Lanka.

www.discoverlk.com/lanka/index.php?option=com_content&view=article&id=294&Itemid=186

This site provides an overview of the classical dances of Sri Lanka, including information about the various forms of dance such as Kandyan dance, Ves Dance, Naiyandi Dance, Uddekki Dance, Pantheru Dance, and more.

www.lanka.com/sri-lanka/arts-and-crafts-of-sri-lanka-103.html

This site contains a summary of arts and crafts in Sri Lanka, including sculpture, painting, architecture, masks, pottery, batik, and jewelry.

LEISURE

Sri Lankan men enjoying a game of *carrom*.

LEISURE

11

LEISURE TIME IS VALUED IN SRI LANKA. School-time lasts only from 8:00 A.M. to 2:00 P.M., after which children can hang out and play.

Working adults pursue recreational activities after office hours and on weekends. In addition there are 24 public holidays. Many women, however, have to juggle household chores, child care, and paid jobs.

Evenings are a popular time for jogging, strolling, swimming, and fishing. The elite, especially in Colombo, play tennis and squash and patronize gymnasiums and health centers. Other Sri Lankans play team sports on the village green or enjoy competitive cycling.

A group of Sri Lankan men relaxing over a game of checkers.

Spectators look on as a giant kite is prepared to be flown.

TRADITIONAL GAMES

Games handed down through generations are played mostly during the April New Year season and at national festivals. A favorite game involves trying to climb a greased pole to retrieve a flag attached to the top. Pillow fights never fail to amuse onlookers. They are fun, and one does not need skill to play. Two players sit astride a pole, with one hand behind their backs, and swipe at each other with a pillow in the other hand. The one who sends the opponent tumbling off the pole wins the game.

Indoor games such as card games, throwing dice, and betting are enjoyed by many Sri Lankans. A favorite indoor game is *panche* (PUNCH-eh), similar to Parcheesi. Instead of dice, *panche* uses seven shells. With the first throw, the shells rest belly down on the ground. Points are earned by moving a marker around the board toward "home." In *olinda kelina* (oh-LIN-dah KAY-li-nah), each player moves red seeds on a low bench with two rows of holes. The aim is to "eat" the opponent's seeds. The first player to deposit all his or her seeds safely in the large hole at one end of the bench wins.

SPORTS

Many Sri Lankans enjoy sports and value the health benefits that come from physical recreation. Social clubs, youth centers, and schools spend a lot of money on developing sports for children and young people, while track and field sports get state funding.

Cricket is the most popular game in Sri Lanka. Sri Lanka's greatest cricketing moment came in the 1996 World Cup, when under the leadership of captain Arjuna Ranatunga, they defeated the top-ranked Australian team in the final. Sri Lanka have maintained a position as one of the top teams of world cricket over the last 20 years, finishing as runners-up in the 2007 and 2011 World Cups, as well as runners-up in the ICC World Twenty20 cricket competition (a shorter version of the game) in 2009. The Sri Lankan cricket team also won the Asia Cup in 1986, 1997, 2004, and 2008.

Children playing cricket on the grassy ramparts of Galle Fort. Cricket is a very popular game in Sri Lanka.

Cycling is popular. Races are often held on public highways, and non-participants run the risk of getting doused with buckets of water meant to cool the cyclists. Tennis and golf have a long history in the country. Soccer is played year-round. The rugby season runs from April to August.

During the cricket season, from January to March, there are the annual interschool cricket matches, such as the Battle of the Blues between the Royal College and Saint Thomas's College. Sri Lanka became a full member of the International Cricket Council in 1982, and the Sri Lankan team won the 1996 World Cup held in the Indian subcontinent.

Sri Lanka has her star athletes, too. Muttiah Muralitharan (b. 1972) is Sri Lanka's most famous cricket star. A specialist bowler with an unorthodox bowling style, Muralitharan holds the world record as the highest wicket-taker in both Test cricket and in One Day Internationals. He retired from international cricket in 2010.

Thuhashini Selvaratnam entered the *Guinness Book of World Records* in 1989 as the youngest person to hold a golf championship title. She was 12 years old.

The Sri Lankan national cricket team (*in blue*) celebrates a win over rival Pakistan.

In 2000 "wonder girl" Susanthika Jayasinghe became the first Sri Lankan woman to win an Olympic medal. She barely missed the silver in the finals of the 200-meter sprint in Sydney and took the bronze instead. Sri Lanka has also fared well in the Asian and South Asian Games and in the Davis Cup tennis tournament.

READING AND TELEVISION

Sri Lanka has a 91 percent literacy rate, among the highest in Asia. Because everyone is interested in political events, reading is the most popular indoor leisure activity. Public library membership is high, and publishing journals and comic books in Sinhala and Tamil is a lucrative business. For those who enjoy watching television, there are several channels: ART TV, TV Derana, Extra Terrestrial Vision (ETV), Independent Television Network, Max TV, MTV Channel, Swarnavahini, Telshan Networks (TNL), TV Lanka, and others.

INTERNET LINKS

www.abyznewslinks.com/srila.htm

This site provides a comprehensive listing of Sri Lanka's media, including local and national newspapers, magazines, and Internet news media.

www.itn.lk/

This is the official website of the Independent Television Network, the pioneer television in Sri Lanka. It includes links to the latest news and programs.

www.lankanewspapers.com/news/lanka_sports_news.jsp

This is the website of the sports news section of LankaNewspapers.com. It includes news items, updates, discussion forums, and more.

FESTIVALS

A Hindu priest makes offerings to a deity during the Munneswaram festival.

12

S RI LANKANS CELEBRATE SO MANY festivals that their year is filled with public holidays. Religious festivals are definite holidays, and each of the four main religious groups—Buddhists, Hindus, Christians, and Muslims—celebrate at least two annual festivals.

In addition there are holidays declared for national anniversaries and monthly full moon *poya* days observed by the Buddhists.

Festivals in Sri Lanka are a cocktail of noise and color. Most have a streak of religious and national fervor. At Vesak, Buddhists brighten their homes and temples with coconut-oil lamps. A religious festival may be enjoyed even by those who do not profess the particular faith. Christmas, for example, is a time of feasting and merrymaking for all.

BUDDHIST FESTIVALS

Vesak, the full moon day in May, commemorates the birth, enlightenment, and death of Siddhartha Gautama, the Buddha. Vesak is essentially a religious festival, austere and devotional more than merry and joyous. Buddhists go to the temple and give the day to worship. Many observe the eight or ten precepts, three or five more than the basic daily requirement, and spend a good part of the day and night in meditation.

Vesak takes on a festive quality after dark. Every home, office, and public place is decorated with strings of light bulbs, candle-lit paper lanterns, or earthen oil lamps. In the big cities, people throng the streets

Here is a glimpse of Sri Lanka's calendar of festivals:

Buddhists observe the poya *day every month. However, the five major full moon days are Duruthu in January, Vesak in May, Poson in June, Esala in August, and Unduvap in December.*

The big Hindu festivals are Thai Pongal in January, Maha Sivarathri in February/ March, Vel in July/August, and Deepavali in October/November.

The Muslim festivals of Ramadan, Haj, and Milad-un-Nabi, the birthday of the Prophet Muhammad, are celebrated in different months in different years, according to the lunar calendar.

Christians in Sri Lanka, as elsewhere, celebrate Christmas in December and Good Friday and Easter in March/April.

In addition Sri Lanka celebrates the following national holidays: Independence Day on February 4 and May Day on May 1. The Sinhalese and Tamil New Year falls in April.

to admire the lights. Open-air theaters attract crowds. The main draw, though, is the *pandal* (PAN-doll).

The *pandal* is a large wooden structure, 60 to 70 feet (18 to 21 m) tall, with painted panels depicting a Jataka tale or a story from the life of the Buddha. The panels are rimmed with rows of little multicolored lights, which blink according to a set pattern. A very large *pandal* uses up to 50,000 bulbs. Music blares forth until the story of the *pandal* is related, also very loudly. Several *dansela* (DHUN-seh-leh), or temporary eating houses, offer free food and soft drinks to passersby.

The *pandal* and *dansela* are funded from collections made throughout the year. Even the poorest tradesman will donate a few rupees, for no one begrudges contributing money toward this important festival. There is no *pandal* in rural areas; Vesak celebrations there are quiet but charming.

Poson, also a major *poya* day, commemorates the introduction of Buddhism in Sri Lanka. *Poson* falls on the full moon day in June,

Lit lanterns at the Vesak festival,

when devotees hold processions all over the country, but especially in Anuradhapura and Mihintale, where Mahinda met King Devanampiya Tissa and preached his first Buddhist sermon.

There are three more major full moon days: Duruthu, Esala, and Unduvap. The other *poya* days, one every month, are celebrated with national as well as religious fervor, though they are essentially days for meditation, simple living, and generous giving.

PERAHERA

In 1775 monks came from Siam (now Thailand) to restore discipline in monasteries in Sri Lanka. While in Kandy, they saw the Esala festival, during which Hindus ask the island's four guardian deities, or *devale*, for protection. The monks protested that Hindu practices were so strong in a country where Buddhism was the established religion. To please the monks, the king of Kandy ordered that the tooth relic of the Buddha be paraded ahead of the *devale*. Thus was born Sri Lanka's most spectacular festival, Kandy's Esala Perahera.

A masked dancer wearing a traditional cobra (*naga raksha*) mask at the Esala Perahera in Colombo.

The Esala Perahera lasts two weeks in July/August. For five nights, dancers, tom-tom beaters, torch bearers, acrobats, and decorated elephants walk in processions in the precincts of the four *devale*—Kataragama, Natha, Vishnu, and Pattini. More elephants join each night, adding color and grandeur to the procession.

On the sixth night, the festival ventures beyond the *devale* precincts. A magnificent temple elephant bearing a howdah (a seat for riding on the back of an elephant or camel) that holds a replica of the tooth relic enters the procession, followed by the chief trustee and other officials of the Dalada Maligawa, or Temple of the Tooth, all dressed in traditional Kandyan court attire.

The seventh night introduces six palanquins carrying ancient jewelry and weapons. Palanquins used to be a mode of travel for women of the aristocracy. The palanquin procession lasts five nights.

The Esala Perahera ends with a water-cutting ceremony. The sword of the Kataragama deity is used to "cut" a circle in the water of a river just outside Kandy. Four earthen pots are filled with water from within the circle. The tooth relic is brought back to the Dalada Maligawa, and each *devale* procession returns to its precinct, bringing along one of the four pots of water, to be kept until the next Esala Perahera.

HINDU FESTIVALS

Most Hindu festivals are celebrated in temples. Besides Thai Pongal, a harvest festival, and Deepavali, the festival of lights, Hindus celebrate several other festivals. The most spectacular is the festival at Kataragama in the south of the island. During this festival in July, many Hindus do penance by passing skewers through their tongue and cheeks, pulling carts attached to hooks in their backs, and balancing on their shoulders a *kavadi*, a semicircular frame covered with red paper and peacock feathers.

A procession takes the head priest bearing the *yantra* (YUN-tra), or relic of the god, to the Valli Amma temple. After a few days the *yantra* is returned to the main Kataragama temple.

The highlight of the Kataragama festival is an awe-inspiring firewalking ceremony. Many Hindu devotees take it as their sacred duty to walk over burning coals to appease the warrior god Skanda. People from all parts of the country, indeed people from other countries, visit Kataragama during the festival to see the firewalkers.

After bathing in the Menik Ganga, or River of Gems, devotees meditate and ask the gods to bless them. They then walk or run across a bed of burning coals, the heat of which can be felt yards away. The firewalkers are believed to be in a special state of mind, as they are able to walk on the coals without getting their soles blistered or burned.

Buddhists also celebrate the Kataragama festival. They pray at the Kiri Vihara temple, then offer flowers and prayers to the god Skanda and smash open a coconut on the ground.

A month or two after the Kataragama festival, the Vel festival is held in Colombo to celebrate the marriage of the god Skanda to his queen, Deivanai. The main streets of Colombo take on a carnival atmosphere during this festival. A beautifully decorated chariot, accompanied by priests and a crowd of devotees, travels a distance of about 6 miles (9.7 km) from the Sea Street temple in Pettah, Colombo's bazaar area, to a temple in Bambalapitiya. The chariot stops frequently to be piled with flowers and other offerings and for people lining the streets to be blessed. Vel is a festive time for everyone in the city. Vendors crowd the streets, offering multicolored bangles, bead necklaces, and bric-a-brac for sale.

Devotees offering clay pots lit with camphor at the Munneswaram festival.

CHRISTIAN FESTIVALS

Santa Claus, fruitcake, wine, carols, and trees covered in bows and lights mark the season of Christmas in Sri Lanka, much as they do in other countries. But to Christians, the true spirit of Christmas is sharing. Catholic families have been encouraged by their priests to take young war victims at a Buddhist orphanage into their homes on Christmas Day. Christian Sri Lankans have responded enthusiastically, some families even asking to have their guest for the whole season.

MUSLIM FESTIVALS

Muslim festivals that are publicly celebrated are Milad-un-Nab—the Prophet Muhammad's birthday and the feast day that ends the fast in the month of Ramadan. *Vatalappan* (VAHT-leh-up-pun), a sweet steamed pudding, and biryani, an aromatic, spicy rice with lamb or chicken, are prepared, and Muslim families share a meal with their non-Muslim friends. Galle Face Green in the heart of Colombo is the site of a mass gathering of Muslim men praying on these festival days.

NEW YEAR

Both Aluth Avuruddha, the Sinhalese New Year, and the Hindu New Year are celebrated in April to mark the sun's entry into the constellation of Aries. They are also harvest festivals, when the major crop is gathered.

Traditions are followed closely. An astrologer dictates the time for all activities. The old year ends at a particular time, when all hearths have to be extinguished. The New Year begins at a prescribed auspicious time, and the hearth is lit again. During the in-between period, the *nonagathe* (non-ah-GAH-thay), no work is to be done. The astrologer advises on what to cook for the first meal (milk rice is the usual main dish), what color the chief female householder should wear, and which direction she should face as she strikes the first match to light the hearth.

Aluth Avuruddha is a time for family closeness, showing respect to elders, gift-giving, feasting, drinking, and playing games. New clothes and furnishings, and even new pots and pans are bought. Swings on trees and giant wheels appear on village threshing fields. Elephant races are held; children start pillow fights. Women play the *rabana* (RAH-bah-neh): they sit around a circular drum with a fire lit underneath and beat the drum in unison.

OTHER CELEBRATIONS

Independence Day is celebrated with parades, dances, and national games. The president raises the national flag opposite the parliament building in Sri Jayewardenepura or at Independence Square, and there is a parade of the armed forces.

On May Day, streets and parks become seas of green, red, blue, and purple—the colors of political parties holding rallies.

INTERNET LINKS

http://hubpages.com/hub/Vesak-Celeberation-in-Sri-Lanka

This is an online article about the significance of Vesak in Sri Lanka and the Buddhist world. It includes external links to other Vesak celebrations.

http://sri-lankan.net/calendar

This site contains a useful online calendar listing all of Sri Lanka's many festivals throughout the year.

www.diwalifestival.org/diwali-in-srilanka.html

This site provides an overview of the Deepavali (also known as Diwali) celebration. It includes information about the history, traditions and customs, meaning and significance, regional significance, and more.

FOOD

A vendor selling produce at the market at Tangalle.

13

THE MOUTH-WATERING AROMAS of the food from the "spice island" can work up anyone's appetite. Sri Lankan curries are loaded with spices, such as tamarind, turmeric, cardamom, cinnamon, coriander, and lemon grass.

Chili pepper—whether green or red, chopped or ground or roasted and powdered, fresh or dried—finds its way into almost any dish. Traditional housewives roast and grind their own spice blends rather than buy ready-packed spices off shop shelves; they claim the latter are not fresh.

RICE AND CURRY

The staple food is rice, eaten with curry. Two other staples are hoppers and stringhoppers, similar to pancakes, the latter resembling a circular pancake made out of netted dough strings. Urbanites have bread for breakfast, with eggs and fruit. On weekends, they may laze over a more traditional breakfast consisting of milk rice and stringhoppers, with *katta sambol* (kut-teh SUM-bole), made of ground red chilies, onions, Maldive fish, and lime.

The dinner staple could be rice, stringhoppers, hoppers, or a local pancake-like bread called *roti* (ROH-ti). There will be at least four curries and one or two side-dishes. The meal is not complete without *badung* (bah-doong), fried dried fish; vegetables with lentils; *malung* (MEHL-loong), finely shredded leaves cooked lightly or served raw; and *papadam* (PAH-peh-doom), a puffy, crisp, spicy wafer.

A typical Sri Lankan meal consists of rice, fried fish, and several vegetable curries.

DRINK

Tea is the most widely drunk beverage in Sri Lanka. The country's finest teas are produced from crops grown above 3,500 feet (1,067 m). Sri Lankans take their tea plain or sweetened, with milk or with a slice of lemon. A popular local version is tea brewed with ginger.

Two other favorite drinks, *tambili* (tam-biee-lee) and *kurumba* (koo-ROOM-bah), are believed to be good for the health. *Tambili* is the water of the orange-hued young coconut; *kurumba* is the water from green coconuts. Cordials are made from many varieties of Sri Lankan fruit—oranges, grapefruit, mangoes, and especially passion fruit. Bottled water and soft drinks are widely available.

Two alcoholic beverages are derived from the coconut palm. Toddy is the fermented sap, and *arrack* (air-rack) is distilled from toddy. The sap of the *kitul* (KI-tool) palm inflorescence yields a sweet toddy rich in vitamins. The tax on *arrack* keeps increasing, encouraging illicit brewers. *Kassippu* (kah-see-poo) is a potent illicit brew.

A man pours toddy, sap from the coconut flower, into a large container to be transported to a toddy bar.

FRUIT

Sri Lanka is a tropical fruit paradise, with varieties to please every taste. Durian, the "king of fruit," is irresistible to some, but repugnant to others with its "rotten" smell, which carries for quite a distance. Mango varieties come in different colors, sizes, and flavors. The color of banana peels may be green, yellow, or reddish-brown. Plantain, a large banana with starchy flesh, is sliced and fried. Pineapple is sometimes added to salads to add piquancy. Wood apples and passion fruit are used to make jams. *Pawpaw*, or papaya, is considered a health food.

A TUTTI-FRUTTI INDUSTRY

Sri Lanka's food-processing industry has been innovative, using the country's wealth of tropical fruit to produce fruit pickles and chutneys, fruit cordials and syrups, fruit jams and marmalades, and dehydrated and canned fruit for both domestic consumption and export. Small-scale enterprises have expanded with the help of the Sri Lanka Agribusiness-Enterprise Project, funded by the United States Agency for International Development.

Mahaweli Canneries, a jam and cordial company west of Colombo, has created a colorful fruit topping for ice cream, cakes, and other desserts. Unripe papayas are first soaked in a sugar solution, and then diced. Different-colored food dyes are added to separate batches of the diced papaya. The stained papaya pieces are next placed in a gas-powered dryer.

The dried pieces of different colors are finally mixed and packed for sale. The company has expanded to produce dehydrated jackfruit and breadfruit as well.

TABLE MANNERS

The traditional way to eat rice and curry is to use the fingers of the right hand to shape little portions of the rice and curry into small balls that can be easily popped into the mouth. It is believed that a Sri Lankan meal tastes better when the diner uses the fingers instead of a fork and spoon. Eating with the fingers is not messy if managed correctly. Properly handled, the food should touch only the fingertips and not get stuck on the lips or beard.

A street food vendor at Dutch Bay.

Villagers often use earthenware vessels as plates and sometimes drink out of polished coconut shells. Ceramic plates and cups, however, are fast replacing traditional utensils. Traditional meals are eaten from leaf mats on the floor. Urbanites sit at the dining table, the focus of social activity in many homes. At mealtimes, the mother usually dishes out the plates of rice. She may then add the curries as well or leave them in separate containers on the table.

FOOD BELIEFS

Sri Lankans have several food taboos. Hindus consider the cow sacred and do not eat beef; many are also vegetarians. Buddhists also avoid eating beef, and Muslims do not eat pork or the meat of animals that have not been slaughtered the Islamic way.

Sinhalese and Tamils believe that some foods are "heaty," while others are "cooling." They say that someone who eats shellfish or "bloodfish," breadfruit, or yellow tuna, for example, may get a redness in the eye. One cools the body by drinking plenty of barley water. There is no clear explanation, however, as to why ice water is considered heaty!

Someone who comes down with chicken pox, mumps, or measles is not allowed to eat any animal product. Instead, the patient gets bland meals consisting of rice and vegetables cooked without chili or saffron.

EATING OUT

Dining out is a family treat. The poor have their *buth kadé* (booth keh-day), or rice shop. In villages, there is the *kopi kadé* (koh-pee keh-day), or coffeeshop, which is more like a social club. On the street, one can look for vendors selling *godamba roti* (GO-dum-ber roh-ti), a paper-thin, square pancake with or without egg.

People in Colombo can dine at restaurants serving Chinese, Japanese, Korean, Thai, French, Swiss, German, and Indian foods, in addition to local cuisine. Besides Western fast-food outlets, such as McDonald's and Pizza Hut, there is also the Indian version, Komala's.

INTERNET LINKS

http://srilankafood.net/

This is the website of Sri Lankan cooking expert Sarogini Kamallanathan, who has been teaching people to cook for more than 20 years. It includes recipes.

www.recipes4us.co.uk/Cooking%20by%20Country/Sri%20Lanka%20 Recipes%20Culinary%20History%20and%20Information.htm

This site provides information on the history and influences of Sri Lankan cooking and cuisine from ancient times to the present day.

www.srilankanrecipes.info/recipes/index.aspx

This site contains a comprehensive collection of delicious Sri Lankan recipes, including meat and vegetable dishes as well as desserts and sweets.

YELLOW RICE

3 cups (710 ml) long grain rice

4 tablespoons (60 ml) butter

2 medium onions, finely sliced

6 whole cloves

20 black peppercorns

3½ teaspoons (17.5 ml) salt

1½ teaspoons (7.5 ml) ground turmeric

5 cups (1.2 l) coconut milk

Wash rice and drain thoroughly. Heat butter in a saucepan. Add onions and fry until golden brown.

Add cloves, peppercorns, salt, and turmeric. Add rice and fry, stirring constantly, until rice is well coated with butter and turmeric. Add coconut milk and bring to a boil. Reduce heat, cover with lid, and cook for another 25 minutes or so, without lifting the lid. When rice is cooked, the spices used will have surfaced to the top. Remove the spices and serve the rice hot with curry.

SRI LANKAN VEGETABLE CURRY

3 medium green chilies, finely chopped

1 medium onion, finely chopped

½ teaspoon (2.5 ml) turmeric

1 stick cinnamon

3 cloves garlic, finely chopped

1 teaspoon (5 ml) ginger, finely chopped

1 teaspoon (5 ml) lemongrass

3 cups (750 ml) coconut milk

2 cups (500 ml) water

Salt to taste

4 cups (1 L) sliced vegetables
  (cabbage, potatoes, zucchini,
  yellow squash, tomatoes)

In a soup pot, combine chilies, onion, turmeric, cinnamon, garlic, ginger, lemongrass, one cup coconut milk, water, and salt. Simmer for 10 minutes. Add vegetables and cook until tender. Add remaining coconut milk. Simmer for 5 minutes. Serve with rice.

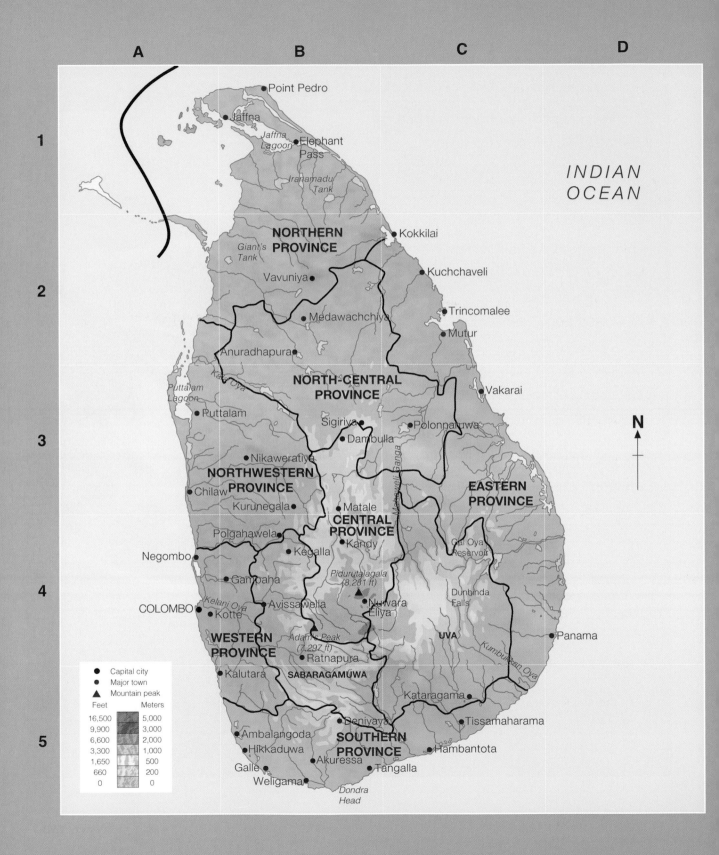

A   B   C   D

1

2

3

4

5

Point Pedro
Jaffna
Jaffna Lagoon
Elephant Pass
Iranamadu Tank

INDIAN
OCEAN

NORTHERN PROVINCE
Giant's Tank
Vavuniya
Kokkilai
Kuchchaveli
Trincomalee
Mutur

Medawachchiya
Anuradhapura
Kala Oya

NORTH-CENTRAL PROVINCE
Vakarai

Puttalam Lagoon
Puttalam
Sigiriya
Dambulla
Polonnaruwa

Nikaweratiya
NORTHWESTERN PROVINCE
Chilaw
Kurunegala

Matale
CENTRAL PROVINCE
Kandy

EASTERN PROVINCE

Mahaweli Ganga

Polgahawela
Kegalla
Negombo
Gambaha
Pidurutalagala (8,281 ft)
Nuwara Eliya

Gal Oya Reservoir
Dunhinda Falls

Kelani Oya
COLOMBO
Kotte
Avissawella
WESTERN PROVINCE
Adam's Peak (7,297 ft)
Ratnapura

UVA
Panama
Kumbukkan Oya

Kalutara
SABARAGAMUWA

Kataragama
Tissamaharama

Deniyaya
SOUTHERN PROVINCE
Hambantota

Ambalangoda
Hikkaduwa
Akuressa
Tangalla
Galle
Weligama
Dondra Head

● Capital city
● Major town
▲ Mountain peak

Feet	Meters
16,500	5,000
9,900	3,000
6,600	2,000
3,300	1,000
1,650	500
660	200
0	0

N

MAP OF SRI LANKA

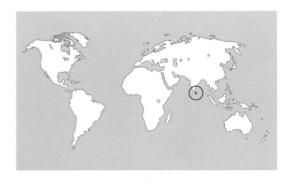

ECONOMIC SRI LANKA

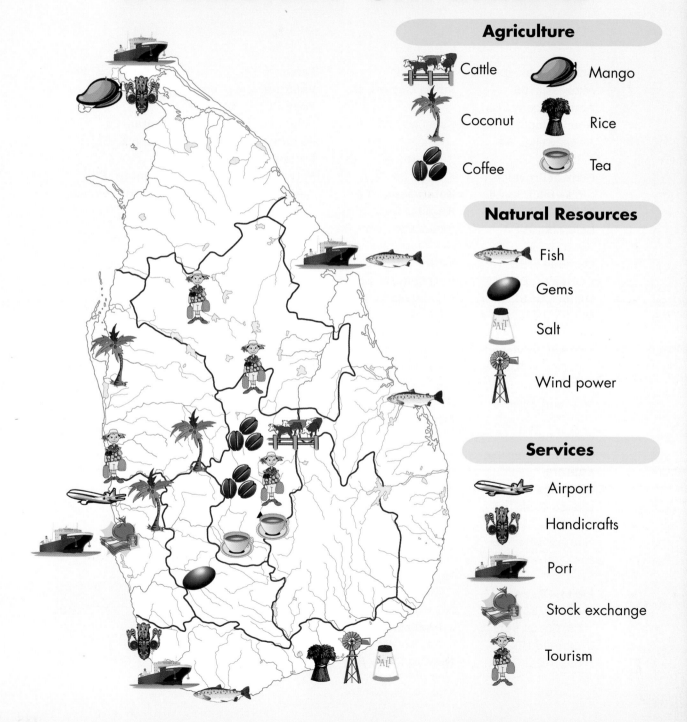

Agriculture

- Cattle
- Coconut
- Coffee
- Mango
- Rice
- Tea

Natural Resources

- Fish
- Gems
- Salt
- Wind power

Services

- Airport
- Handicrafts
- Port
- Stock exchange
- Tourism

ABOUT THE ECONOMY

OVERVIEW

After 26 years of civil war, which ended in 2009, Sri Lanka reported a growth of 3.5 percent in the same year. Major investments in rebuilding and development projects are taking place, including enhancing the country's electrical supplies and reconstructing its transportation systems. The global financial crisis of 2008 and 2009, which affected many stronger economies around the world, did not help Sri Lanka. Fortunately a $2.6 billion package from the IMF in 2009 helped support the country's fragile economy. Today the Colombo stock market (CSE) is recognized as one of the world's top performing markets.

GROSS DOMESTIC PRODUCT (GDP)

$49.68 billion (2010 estimate)

LAND USE

Arable land 13.96 percent, permanent crops 15.24 percent, other 70.8 percent (2005)

AGRICULTURAL PRODUCTS

Rice, sugarcane, grains, pulses, oilseed, spices, vegetables, fruit, tea, rubber, coconuts, milk, eggs, hides, beef, fish

CURRENCY

USD 1 = LKR 113.90 (January 2012)
1 Sri Lankan rupee (LKR) = 100 cents

WORKFORCE

8.1 million (2010)

LABOR FORCE BY OCCUPATION

Agriculture: 32.7 percent; Industry: 26.3 percent; Services: 41 percent (2008 estimate)

UNEMPLOYMENT RATE

5.4 percent (1999)

MAJOR EXPORTS

Textiles and apparel, tea and spices, rubber manufactures, precious stones, coconut products, fish

MAJOR IMPORTS

Petroleum, textiles, machinery and transportation equipment, building materials, mineral products, foodstuffs

MAJOR TRADING PARTNERS

India, China, Singapore, Iran (2009)

MAJOR PORTS

Sea ports at Colombo, Galle, Trincomalee (natural harbor); Katunayake International Airport

INTERNATIONAL PARTICIPATION

Commonwealth of Nations; Non-Aligned Movement (NAM); South Asian Association for Regional Cooperation (SAARC); United Nations Educational, Scientific, and Cultural Organization (UNESCO); World Intellectual Property Organization (WIPO)

CULTURAL SRI LANKA

Holy City
The remains of the ancient city of Anuradhapura are visited by Buddhist pilgrims every year. The city was built around a fig tree started from a cutting from the tree under which the Buddha attained enlightenment. The oldest temple here is believed to house the Buddha's right collarbone. Anuradhapura, with its ancient temples and palaces, has been declared a World Heritage Site by UNESCO.

Esala Perahera
Kandy is the home of the Temple of the Tooth, which houses the sacred Tooth Relic of the Buddha. Pilgrims visit the relic every day, amid drumming and chanting. During the Esala Perahera, a festival in July/August, an elephant carries a casket containing a replica of the sacred tooth through the streets in a colorful parade of decorated elephants, drummers, and dancers.

Elephant Orphanage
The Pinnewela Elephant Orphanage was set up by the government as a home for baby elephants found in the wild with no mother. The elephants can roam freely in the orphanage, and keepers bathe and feed them at regular times.

City of Gems
Ratnapura is the center of Sri Lanka's gem industry. Rubies, sapphires, topaz, amethysts, aquamarines, garnets, zircons, and other gems are mined, cut, and polished in Ratnapura and exported to countries around the world.

Sinharaja Forest Reserve
The only remaining expanse of virgin tropical rain forest in the Sri Lankan lowlands, the Sinharaja forest is home to many endemic species of plants and animals. The forest was declared a biosphere reserve in 1978 and a Natural World Heritage Site in 1988.

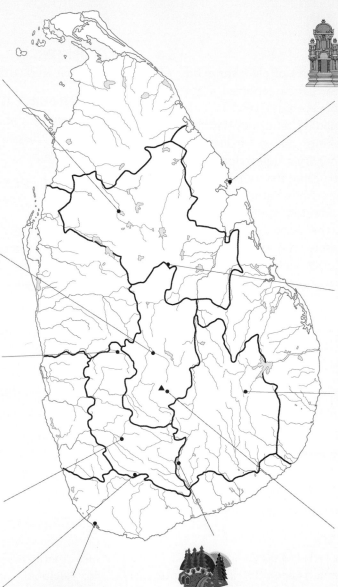

Old Dutch Fort
At the old Dutch fort in Galle are Dutch houses, museums, churches, and the New Oriental Hotel, built for Dutch governors in 1684.

Uda Walawe National Park
This park was established to protect the Uda Walawe reservoir and to provide a new home for animals displaced by the Walawe River Development Scheme. The park has elephants, wildcats, fox, bears, monkeys, wild pigs, leopards, spotted deer, snakes, butterflies, and birds such as the rare-faced malkoha.

Swami Rock
Trincomalee is the site of a huge rock known as Swami Rock, on which lie the ruins of the ancient Temple of a Thousand Columns. The temple was the largest of at least three built on the rock by Hindus, but it was destroyed in 1624 by the Portuguese, who built a fort in its place. Both Hindus and Buddhists today venerate this site, bringing fruit and flower offerings every year.

Lion Mountain
Sigiriya is an ancient city with water and boulder gardens and cave paintings. At the top of Lion Mountain—a rock rising 656 feet (200 m)—are the remains of an old fortress.

Dunhinda Falls
One of Sri Lanka's most beautiful waterfalls, though not one of its tallest, the Dunhinda gets its name from the mist it creates (*dun* means "mist") as the water falls from a height of 210 feet (60 m).

Lovers' Leap
Legend has it that two lovers, not allowed to be together, jumped to their death at this waterfall, hence its name. Lovers' Leap begins in the south slope of Pidurutalagala, Sri Lanka's highest mountain, and can be seen from Nuwara Eliya.

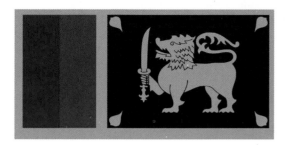

OFFICIAL NAME
The Democratic Socialist Republic of Sri Lanka

CAPITAL
Colombo

GOVERNMENT
Democratic government with executive president and 225-member parliament

DESCRIPTION OF FLAG
On the right-hand side of the Sri Lankan flag is a crimson block with a yellow sword-bearing lion. On the left are two vertical bands, one green and one orange. The flag symbolizes the independence yet unity of the major ethnic groups: the lion represents the Sinhalese, believed to be descended from a lion; the green band represents the Moors; and the orange band represents the Tamils. In the corners of the crimson area are four bo leaves that stand for universal love, kindness, joy, and equanimity.

POPULATION
21,283,913 (2011 estimate)

LIFE EXPECTANCY
75.73 years (male 72.21, female 79.38) (2011)

LITERACY RATE
90.7 percent (male 92.3 percent, female 89.1 percent) (2001 census)

ETHNIC GROUPS
Sinhalese 73.8 percent, Sri Lankan Moors 7.2 percent, Indian Tamil 4.6 percent, Sri Lankan Tamil 3.9 percent, other 0.5 percent, unspecified 10 percent (2001 census provisional data)

RELIGIONS
Buddhist 69.1 percent, Muslim 7.6 percent, Hindu 7.1 percent, Christian 6.2 percent, unspecified 10 percent (2001 census provisional data)

OFFICIAL LANGUAGES
Sinhala and Tamil

NATIONAL HOLIDAYS
Thai Pongal, National Day, Sinhalese and Tamil New Year, Good Friday, Vesak, Poson, Deepavali, Christmas, Milad-un-Nabi, Id-ul-Fidr

LEADERS IN POLITICS
Don Stephen Senanayake—first prime minister
J. R. Jayewardene—first president
Sirimavo R. D. Bandaranaike—world's first woman prime minister

TIME LINE

IN SRI LANKA	IN THE WORLD
	1206–1368 Genghis Khan unifies the Mongols and starts conquest of the world. At its height, the Mongol Empire under Kublai Khan stretches from China to Persia and parts of Europe and Russia.
1505 The Portuguese arrive.	
1521 Royal capital moves to Sitawaka; Kandyan kingdom gains power.	
1606 The Dutch arrive.	
1638 The Dutch expel the Portuguese.	
	1776 U.S. Declaration of Independence
1796 British East India Company is established.	**1789–99** The French Revolution
1802 Ceylon becomes a British Crown colony.	
1815 Ceylon is unified under British rule.	**1914** World War I begins.
1931 Universal suffrage is granted to men and women over 21 years of age.	**1939** World War II begins.
	1945 The United States drops atomic bombs on Hiroshima and Nagasaki. World War II ends.
1948 Independence from British rule	
1972 Sri Lanka becomes a republic.	
1983 Liberation Tigers of Tamil Eelam wage war in the north and east.	
1988 Ranasinghe Premadasa is elected president.	
1993 President Premadasa is assassinated.	
1994 Chandrika Kumaratunga is elected president.	**1997** Hong Kong is returned to China.

IN SRI LANKA	IN THE WORLD

1998
A Tamil Tiger suicide bombing devastates the Temple of the Tooth, killing 13 people.

2001
Tamil Tigers attack the Bandaranaike International Airport, blowing up six aircraft and killing 21 people. Ranil Wickremesinghe becomes the prime minister.

2001
Terrorists crash planes into New York, Washington D.C., and Pennsylvania.

2002
The government and the Tamil Tigers sign a ceasefire agreement. Peace talks begin.

2003
War in Iraq begins.

2004
More than 30,000 people are killed in the Indian Ocean tsunami.

2004
Eleven Asia countries are hit by giant tsunami, killing at least 225,000 people.

2005
The foreign minister is killed by a suspected Tamil Tiger assassin. Prime Minister Mahinda Rajapaksa wins the presidential elections.

2005
Hurricane Katrina devastates the Gulf Coast of the United States.

2006
Attacks begin to escalate, and government forces and Tamil Tiger fighters resume fighting in the northeast.

2008
Suicide bombers kill 27 people. Fighting between government forces and the Tamil Tigers continues.

2008
Earthquake in Sichuan, China, kills 67,000 people.

2009
Government troops capture the northern town of Kilinochchi, held for 10 years by the Tamil Tigers as their headquarters.

2009
Outbreak of flu virus H1N1 around the world

2010
Sitting president Mahinda Rajapaksa wins presidential election.

2011
Twin earthquake and tsunami disasters strike northeast Japan, leaving over 14,000 dead and thousands more missing.

GLOSSARY

bo tree
Latin name of tree is *Ficus religiosa*. Prince Siddhartha sat under one in Gaya, India, when he attained enlightenment and gave the world the philosophy of Buddhism.

caste
A system categorizing people according to their profession. Tamils and Sinhalese have their own forms of the caste system.

***dagoba* (DAH-go-beh)**
A Buddhist shrine containing sacred relics of the Buddha or his disciples.

***devale* (DAY-vah-leh)**
A Hindu deity, or a Hindu temple containing an image of the god worshiped within.

***dhoby* (DHOH-bee)**
A person who washes others' clothes and linen.

***ganga* (GUNG-gah)**
A river.

***kovil* (KOH-vil)**
A Hindu shrine.

***magul kapuwa* (MAH-gool KAH-poo-wah)**
A traditional broker of arranged marriages.

***namaste* (neh-MEHS-tay)**
A gesture of greeting, in which the person bows slightly with the palms of both hands pressed together in front of the chest.

***perahera* (PAIR-ah-HAIR-ah)**
An elaborate procession of elephants. Major temples have annual *perahera*. Sri Lanka's biggest *perahera* takes place in Kandy.

***poya* (POH-yeh)**
A Buddhist holy day, the monthly full moon. There are five major ones: Duruthu in January, Vesak in May, Poson in June, Esala in August, and Unduvap in December.

***sarama* (SAH-rah-mah)**
An ankle-length sarong worn by Sinhalese men.

sari
A large piece of cloth wound around the waist and shoulder. It is worn by Sinhalese and Tamil women, with a blouse and long slip.

***sil* (sil)**
Observation of the eight or ten Buddhist precepts. A lay Buddhist keeps five precepts daily.

toddy
A beverage with a fair alcoholic content. It is the fermented sap of the talipot or coconut palm inflorescence.

***vihare* (VI-haar-eh)**
A Buddhist temple.

***wewa* (WAY-weh)**
An irrigation tank, or man-made lake for collecting and storing water for rice fields.